ENVISN

ENVISN

A SIMPLE GUIDE
TO LIVING A
FANATICALLY ABUNDANT LIFE

SHANE PERRY SR.

W

WHITAKER
HOUSE

ENVISION
A Simple Guide to Living a Fanatically Abundant Life

www.drshaneperry.com

ISBN: 978-1-64123-005-6
eBook ISBN 978-1-62911-991-5
Printed in the United States of America
© 2018 by Shane Perry Sr.

Whitaker House
1030 Hunt Valley Circle
New Kensington, PA 15068
www.whitakerhouse.com

Library of Congress Cataloging-in-Publication Data
LC record available at https://lccn.loc.gov/2018020881

1 2 3 4 5 6 7 8 9 10 11 ⊔⅃ 25 24 23 22 21 20 19 18

CONTENTS

INTRODUCTION

INTRODUCTION

Understanding vision and how it works is one of the most important steps to living a truly fulfilling life. Too many of us are living below our God-given potential. We have gifts lying dormant, just waiting to be unleashed. We have untapped power that we have yet to access. Many of us feel as if life is passing us by as we do all we can just to survive. We often daydream of a better life, only to have it interrupted by the nightmare of our everyday experience.

If you're tired of the unlived life and feel that you were put on earth for a greater purpose, then you have picked up the right book. I want to call to that inner voice that tells you more is possible. That greatness is within all of us, just waiting to be activated. I want to offer you a simple guide to a seemingly difficult subject of vision.

> Too many of us are living below our God-given potential. We have gifts lying dormant, just waiting to be unleashed. We have untapped power that we have yet to access. Many of us feel as if life is passing us by as we do all we can just to survive.

I was always told throughout my life that I needed to get a vision or some variation of this concept. People would ask me questions about my life. What are your plans? Do you have goals? What's your strategy? I didn't have the answers because no one had ever instructed me on how to lay out a plan for my life. I was purposeless, and I didn't know how to find my place. I can remember my senior year of high school—as the year came to an end, I became depressed. I was depressed because I knew that I had to find a life. How do you chart out your course as an eighteen-year-old (or, in my case, a nineteen-year-old, because I failed the eighth grade)? All I had was sports and a GPA just high enough to keep me eligible to stay on the football field or the wrestling mat. I didn't have a plan for college because I didn't work hard enough in school to qualify. I figured I would go to junior college, but I had no idea what to major in. As the depression sunk in, I felt even more powerless to control my future.

I took a job to stay busy while I tried to figure it all out. I knew that I didn't want to work in the steel mills that my family worked in, besides, all that work was leaving Birmingham, Alabama, as the Japanese became the main steel producers. I had seen people around me seemingly work themselves to death with nothing to show for it. I didn't know what I wanted to do, but I knew I didn't want to live a mundane life. I couldn't see myself staying in the same town following the same old patterns as generations before me. I was not putting anyone down or the value of hard work, but I just felt like there was something more. There was a different way to live, a way that served a purpose.

Once I got saved (which I'll talk about in more detail later), I came in contact with the master of my destiny, and it was there that my life began to take shape. It's interesting to note that even after my conversion experience, I still struggled to get my vision off the ground and doubted if it would ever happen. Proverbs 13:12 says, *"Hope deferred makes the heart sick: but when the desire comes, it is a tree of life"* (AKJV). Life has a way of challenging your vision, pushing beyond your limits, and challenging you on all levels. It's as if every vision has to go through the crucible of struggle to make sure you really want it. When something is delayed, it can bring feelings of disappointment and can make you quite insecure when it comes to God's ability to perform. I have found myself in a place of doubt because it seemed as if my life was going in the opposite direction of vision. It's important during these times to understand that it's all a part of the process and if you don't stop, you can't lose. When you allow yourself to dream big, you will undoubtedly have your hope tested. You will experience the sick heart that comes with wanting something so bad only to have it drawn out sometimes for years. If you keep your focus on your desire, it will ultimately be a tree of life to you.

I know what it's like to step out in faith—to dream beyond my means and my abilities. I know what it's like to feel as if it will never happen. I also know what it feels like to see a dream actually manifest in my life. That's what this book is all about—taking what I've learned and experienced in my life as it relates to vision and sharing that with you. You have no excuse! Everything you need is within you, regardless of your perceived limitations. I want you to know that nothing can stop you but you.

> Everything you need is within you, regardless of your perceived limitations. I want you to know that nothing can stop you but you.

I recently went to a business seminar, and one of the presenters was missing both his legs and had only one arm, which was damaged. He began his presentation by listing all the things he had accomplished, including scuba diving, wrestling, skateboarding, and obtaining a contract as a fitness model with a major supplement company. His message was simple: He felt as if he was put here on earth to show able-bodied people that if he could reach his goals, they could too; nothing is impossible for us. I have been blessed to experience incredible things in my life, but as I listened to him, I slowly realized that there is so much more I could accomplish if I set my mind to it and put action to my thoughts.

You're limited only by what you think. You have to see yourself going beyond what you are currently doing with your life. I want to call you to a higher place. I want to summon within you that great power of purpose and ignite the vision God has for your life. There are no special people who magically live life on purpose. You have to set your mind and your actions on a target and follow that path all the way through to the end. I want to help you reach your ultimate goals and live a life of fulfillment.

I wrote this book because I want to put in your hands a powerful tool that will give you everything you need to find success in life—success as God defines it for you. Third John 1:2 (AKJV) says, "*I wish above all things that you may prosper and be in health, even as your soul prospers.*" God's design for your life is to experience a prosperous, fanatically abundant life. God wants to do more than just supply your needs. He wants to cause you to live in a place of more than enough, of overflow. He also wants you to be healthy. So many of us have lived on the roller coaster of sickness and healing and have never experienced God's health-care plan. Will you have health challenges? Sure, all of us do. But you can overcome and live a healthy life. God put you on this planet to enjoy your life, and you can't do that if you're sick all the time.

Last, He wants you to have balanced emotions and a sound mind. So many of us have been wounded and have suffered emotional pain because of our wounds. We've been let down by family members, friends, and relationships, and, oftentimes, we feel all alone. We come to our defining moments with emotional baggage that can hinder us from maximizing our time when the vision and manifestation collide.

As we learn to construct our vision according to God's plan for our lives, we will learn how to write a vision that covers every area of our lives. You'll learn how to write a vision for your ideal weight and optimal health. You'll discover how to heal from the pain of your past and experience true freedom. Finally, you'll set financial goals, whether that means being debt-free or financially independent and secure. The great thing about writing out your vision is that you are free to deal with any aspect of your life that you want to change.

You can do more with the time you have left. Regardless of your age, you can follow your dreams. It doesn't matter what has happened before. Maybe you've tried all of this before, and it didn't work out for you. So, here you are, jaded and afraid to step out again. The question is, at what cost? Do you want to just exist, or coexist with God's original design for your life? If you read this book with an open mind and an intention that you will break out and live the life of your dreams, then you can see the fulfillment of your highest aspirations and enjoy your life.

Of course, there will be bumps along the way and lessons to be learned, but if you stick to your plan, you will see incredible results. I have learned more from my failures than I have ever learned from my successes. You may ask why this is. It's simple—I've had more of them. That's right, I've had so many failures, bumps, and bruises. I've missed the mark more than I've hit it. Yet each time I missed, I was able to recalibrate and try again with greater accuracy the next time.

I think one of the major lessons of vision is to continue to show up. I remember the words of my platoon sergeant, who was also one of my greatest mentors. He said that when you show up, you've done more than most people are willing to do. These words never rang truer than when I went before the promotion board. My first-line supervisor had been demoted, my mentor had been temporarily taken off his post, and I had preached the night before and had lost my voice. So here I was, with no voice and no one to go to the board with me, which is a requirement when you go before the board. So, what did I do? I showed up. When I showed up to the promotion board with a voice that was barely louder a whisper and no representation, it was as if the board knew what I was up against. They were so impressed that instead of drilling me with questions, they asked me only one. I remember it so clearly:

"Perry, where are you from?"

I said, "Alabama."

They all gave me a special coin that high-ranking leaders carry to acknowledge a job well done, and I passed the board on one question. That's the power of showing up! If you keep showing up, you'll see your relationships turn for the better. If you keep showing up, you'll find your health improving. If you keep showing up, your persistence will attract everything that God had planned for you to have before you ever came into this world.

> If you keep showing up, your persistence will attract everything that God had planned for you to have before you ever came into this world.

The title of this book came to me while I was already writing. The word *envision* just seemed to embody the essence of what this work was all about. According to dictionary.com, *envision* means "to picture mentally, especially some future event or events: to envision a bright future."[1] This is exactly what I'm asking of you as you apply the principles of this book. There is no secret, no magical potion—just time-tested biblical principles that work if you use them.

I immediately related this word to one of my favorite Scriptures in the Bible. Psalm 133:1 says, *"Behold, how good and how pleasant it is for brethren to dwell together in unity!"* (ASV). In Christian circles, this verse has always been used during unity-style services. It's often used when multiple churches get together to worship as one large group. I believe, however, that this diminishes the original intent of this verse. Most theologians agree that David wrote this psalm before he became the unified king of Israel; he was thinking about the time when he would rule over a unified kingdom when he wrote it. So, imagine, if you will, David. He's been running from King Saul, who's not about to release the throne with ease. David found himself surrounded by people who were in trouble with the law, in debt, and, basically, vagabonds. David practices his leadership skills on this group of undesirables and proves himself with them. Perhaps David's greatest feat wasn't becoming the king but being able to take a group of thieves and turn them into an army.

---

1. "envision," *Dictionary.com*, http://www.dictionary.com/browse/envision?s=t.

David understood the concept of reaching the lost, which was the backdrop of Psalm 133. Here was David, standing with this group, and he spoke what he saw. He said, in essence, how good it was going to look when God brought everything together. The word *"behold"* is another word for vision. *Vision* is translated from Hebrew word *chazon*. This word means a mental sight, dream, or revelation. So just like David, we have the power to get a divine revelation of our future, allow it to become a mental picture, and speak it as if we already have it. It doesn't matter what you start with, just that you get started. If you give it enough time and attention, it will work in your favor, but you must first envision what you want.

As you turn the pages of this book, I will unlock for you the truths of vision from a biblical and practical standpoint, and guide you on a simple path to finding God's ultimate vision for your life. You will have at your disposal tested truths about vision. If you write your vision, speak your vision, and plan for the success of your vision, you will see amazing things happen. I invite you to take off the restraints and allow yourself to see something greater than what is in your life right now. Follow the pattern I lay out before you and prepare yourself for an amazing shift in your life. I hope you're ready to experience God's best for your life by following these biblical principles, which are guaranteed to yield positive results in your life.

IT WORKED FOR ME

ONE

IT WORKED FOR ME

I will never forget that cold day in Alabama. I was lying on my mother-in-law's floor with tears streaming down my face. I was broke, homeless, and about to lose everything I owned. I thought to myself, *How in the world did I get here?* And, even more importantly, *How am I going to get out of this predicament?*

A month prior to this time, I had been living in northern California. I had moved there in hopes of starting a successful ministry in evangelism as I worked with a local church. But I had not been able to get things moving in the right direction. My wife was pregnant with our first child, and we found ourselves in a very difficult situation. We were on government assistance—the Special Supplemental Nutrition Program for Women, Infants, and Children (WIC), as well as food stamps. It was a very trying time for us. When we could no longer make payments on our apartment, and we were forced to move. We put all our household goods in storage in hopes of shipping them to us when we found a new place to live. We traveled back to our home town of Birmingham, Alabama, and moved in with my mother-in-law, trying to pick up the pieces.

When we moved back, we both tried to get jobs and had a very difficult time. My wife had to strap her stomach down because she was showing and trying to get hired, and I was looking for work as well. Of course, if we didn't do something, one of our cars would be towed when our parking permit at the apartment expired, and all our stuff would be auctioned off if we didn't have it shipped.

So here I was, laying on the floor in one of the two suits I had brought with me from California, wearing a leather jacket that didn't fit, and wondering what my next move would be.

On that day, I asked God a very pointed question: "Lord, I know nothing is wrong with You, so what's wrong with me?"

The answer came back so clearly: "You lost your dream."

I knew at that exact moment what that meant. When I was nine-teen years old, I had attended a large meeting in Memphis, Tennessee, at the Church of God in Christ. Sitting in the nosebleed section of the Memphis Cook Convention Center, I'd received a clear vision. I'd known that, one day, I would stand on that stage and preach.

Lying on that floor, I began to feel an overwhelming excitement that this could still happen. Even though I was thirty-three years old, I realized that the dream could still come to pass. I also thought about all the things that could happen, and I decided to take the limits off of what I thought was possible. I made a conscious choice that I was going to allow myself to dream and to dream big.

After working through the principles of vision for a few months, I decided that I needed to do what Habakkuk 2:2 instructs: "*Write the vision, and make it plain*" (ASV). I bought a notebook and began to think about and write down how my life could look in a multitude of areas. I was homeless, but I started dreaming about a big house. I was broke, but I envisioned what wealth would look like for me. I figured that nothing was wrong with dreaming, and dream I did. I wrote down what I wanted to happen in my future in all areas of my life. Let's take a look at what happened in two of the areas I wrote about.

Envisioning a Home

One of the things I wrote in my vision was that I would have a million-dollar house "over the mountain." To people who live in Birmingham, "over the mountain" is a colloquialism for one of the wealthier sides of town. I remember thinking that it probably wouldn't happen, but what could it hurt to envision? I described in great detail what my house would look like. I wanted a multilevel home, a Jacuzzi in the bedroom, a pool, multiple car garages, and a view. (Anyone who knows me knows that I'm all about a great view! The first thing I do when I enter a hotel is pull open the curtains and look at the view.)

Something strange happened as I wrote this vision out—I started to feel like I was on to something. I felt like maybe this could actually work, which was followed directly by a rush of doubt about its possibility. (It always amazes me how we have to wrestle with our deep-seated fears whenever we start to dream.) Nevertheless, I continued to write. I took this detailed description and turned it into a goal. I wrote, "Million-dollar home over the mountain." It was short and simple but easy to wrap my mind around. I knew I had the details written out in my description, but I needed something to work with.

The next thing I did was write a confession for my goal. I wrote on a separate page, "I am now succeeding at having a million-dollar home over the mountain." Faith is always spoken in the now, but it also needs something true. So, I may not have actually had it then, but by faith I did. The word *succeeding* gives the impression that you're working on something, which is important in the vision process. That's why the Bible says in James 2:7 that faith without works (action) is dead. After I wrote out my confession, which I immediately began to speak throughout the day, I knew I needed a plan. I wrote down my plan for accomplishing my goal on a new sheet of paper. It's so important to know that, without a plan, there is no true action. Your plan sets a collision course between you and your goals.

It's so important to know that, without a plan, there is no true action. Your plan sets a collision course between you and your goals.

Once I did all this, I continued to speak this every day, completely oblivious to what was about to happen. About two weeks after writing out my vision, I was in a church service in Birmingham at a convention they were hosting. I remember so vividly the preacher asking for a special offering after he preached. His requested amount was five hundred dollars, and I remember thinking he was crazy. He even made the bold statement that there were twenty-one people who could give that amount. I said to myself that there was no way I was giving that offering. I will never forget this as long as I live, because I clearly heard the voice of the Lord. He said to me, "Yes you are." I thought to myself that I didn't even have the money. I was *going* to have it, because I was going to be paid that amount that Friday for a job I had recently gotten. With much reluctance, I stood up with a pledge to give it when I got paid, a pledge I upheld. Once I stood up with this seed, the preacher looked at me and said, "You're going to move into your dream house this year." I thought to myself how amazing it was that I had just written out a vision for my house and that this man was calling out exactly what I had written down.

My doubts began to lessen, but I was still so far away from this coming to pass. I was struggling financially, I was about to lose all I owned, I was wondering where my next meal would come from, and I had just given away my check for that week—not to mention my credit was terrible. Yet that vision started talking to me. Habakkuk backs this up because the aforementioned Scripture, which says, *"I will…look forth to see what he will speak with me"* (Habakkuk 2:1). The vision was getting louder in my spirit, and I started to wonder how this would all come together.

The next day, my wife called me and said that she had been searching for houses that we could afford (which wasn't much) and that she found a man with several houses in our price range that we could possibly rent. She also told me that he had this one amazing home listed with the others, but I blew her off and focused on the houses that cost seven hundred dollars per month. She gave me his number and asked me to call him.

When I did, he and I had a wonderful conversation. I found out that he was a preacher from California. We talked at length about the Bible, and he asked me to lunch. While at lunch, he asked if I would like to see his houses. We drove around and looked at several of his homes. Afterward, he asked me where my wife was. He took me to pick her up, and we drove up on a mountain over the mountain! We pulled into a 7,500-square-foot home with everything I had listed in my vision, including a view! As we walked through the house, he talked about how we could put certain items in the house and asked my wife what she thought. What happened next still amazes me after all these years.

A few hours after we left, he called us. His instructions were simple: "Come to my house. I have something to tell you".

My wife and I immediately stopped what we were doing and went directly to his house. He brought us into his office and sat us in front of him and asked me a simple question. These were his exact words: "Yes or no—do you want this house?"

With a vision I had written out two weeks prior, a seed I had put in the ground, and a word that I would move into my dream home, you would think that I would answer with a definitive yes, but I didn't. I asked what it would cost me for the down payment plus the monthly rent, which both were extremely expensive. I obviously missed the moment, and I'm sure my wife wanted to kick me under the table.

He retorted, "I didn't ask you that! Yes or no—do you want this house?"

I finally answered in the affirmative.

He slid a modified contract across the table and told us to have the power turned on in our name. We moved into a million-dollar house with no money and no credit. What I had written down, "Million-dollar house over the mountain," came to pass before my very eyes!

I remember when we moved in, we looked around and tried to figure out how we could furnish such a big house. I looked at my wife and told her to do what we had done to get the house—I told her to speak what she wanted to each room. A couple of days later, the man came to our door and looked around. He told my wife and me to follow him. We went to the furniture store, and he furnished the house for us. Psalm 112:3 says, *"Wealth and riches shall be in his house."* So God not only gave us the house but He also filled it with furniture! I don't tell this story to brag or out of a spirit of hubris; in fact, I am always humbled by God's tremendous power to work through a vision when I share it with others.

> What's the factor that determines what happens in each individual's life? It's simple. You have to be willing to get a God-inspired vision for your life and follow through on what you write down on paper.

I remember cleaning out and filling up the pool when we moved in. I always wanted a pool, and the first time I went for a swim, tears streamed down my face because I was seeing God do something so supernatural in my life. The thing to remember is that Romans 2:11 tells us that God is *"no respecter of persons."* God doesn't regard one person above another. So, what's the factor that determines what happens in each individual's life? It's simple. You have to be willing to get a God-inspired vision for your life and follow through on what you write down on paper. That's the difference! You have dreamers that who stick with their vision no matter what happens and those who will encounter the inevitable twists and turns of a vision and give up before the manifestation. I want to show you how to write your vision, speak your vision, plan for the success of your vision, and allow God to bring it all to pass in your life.

Envisioning My Ministry

The next part of my vision that I saw manifest involved my ministry. Do you remember the first thing God had spoken to me while I was lying on my mother-in-law's floor? I was immediately reminded of the original dream God had given me. I was taken back to that seat in the highest bleacher of the Memphis Cook Convention Center. Among thousands of people and at the age of nineteen, I'd known that I would someday preach on that stage.

The same vision I'd written out for the house, I'd written out for this defining moment in my life. I'd written out in great detail how it would all happen, and it all happened that way. This one took about a year to come to pass, but it was another incredible unfolding of God's power working through the vision He had given to me. I knew there had to be a path to this monumental vision, so I asked God to give me a plan. I had met the leader of the Church of God in Christ while I was stationed in California while I was in the army, but I didn't have an established relationship with him. I also thought of the marketing director of the church, who is now one of its top leaders, and knew that if I could meet him and somehow let him hear me speak, he would give me a chance as well. So I wrote in my plan that I would become reacquainted with Bishop Blake and meet Bishop Brandon Porter.

I had begun working for the church in Birmingham I originally came out of, and my pastor was a bishop as well. I was put in charge of bringing in speakers for our conference. During one of our conferences, I was asked to bring in Bishop Porter. When I first met him, we had a very good conversation about ministry, and he seemed interested in my preaching. A few months later, I was in Memphis, where he pastors, and he gave me an opportunity to speak. After hearing me speak, I remember him saying, "Where have you been? Why hasn't anyone given you an opportunity?"

The next speaker we brought in was the leader of the pastor's counsel. I was assigned to pick him up from the airport. He was on the phone the entire time from the time he got off the plane to the car. I overheard him say that he was in Birmingham, and the person on the other end mentioned my name. I know this because he said to me, "Are you Shane Perry?"

I replied yes.

Then he said, "Here, Brandon Porter wants to talk to you."

So the entire time he was on the phone, he was talking to the person I had written about in my vision and had just preached for! Of course, Bishop Porter told him about my ministry, and before the summer was over, I was speaking in front of all the pastors in the church.

The last speaker we brought in for the year was Bishop Blake himself. I will never forget the instruction I was given when I was leaving to escort him to the airport the following morning. The Holy Spirit spoke to me and told me to get a DVD of the last time I spoke at Evangel Church of God in Christ in North Carolina with the late Bishop Otis Lockett. (You can't go wrong with Lockett in your pocket!) The DVD didn't have a label on it, and the only case I had was light pink. Nevertheless, I grabbed it and put it in my jacket pocket.

When I got into the vehicle with the bishop, he looked up at me and said, "You know I've heard that you are a good preacher. Will you send a DVD to my office?"

I said to him, "You know, bishop, I just so happen to have one with me right now." I reached into my pocket and put that DVD right in the man's hand.

A couple of months after this exchange, I received an email from the national church asking me to be a speaker in the upcoming convocation. The amazing thing was that this was the last year it was held in Memphis. The very next year, it was moved to St. Louis, which shows God's perfect timing. His word to me was that I would stand on stage at the Memphis Cook Convention Center, and that November, that's exactly what happened. Through the power of God's vision for my life, I watched the events play out perfectly, and my dream happened! Amazingly, I was also given the opportunity to speak in the first convocation held in St. Louis the next year. Since that time, I have preached in some of the largest conferences and churches in the country and abroad. It all began with the boldness to write down what I knew God wanted to do in my life.

As you turn the pages of this book, I want to help you unlock your deepest desires—the things that God has placed in your very soul. I want to you to free yourself to dream the grandest dream you can imagine, and give you the tools to see it come to fruition. No one is more favored or special than another person. You can achieve your dreams and live the vision God has for your life.

VISION BEGINS WITH GOD

TWO

VISION BEGINS WITH GOD

Probably one of the most asked questions when dealing with vision is "How do I find out what God wants for my life?" I have discovered that some people seem to be born knowing what they want to do with their lives, and others struggle to find their purpose and meaning. I can remember as a child being fascinated by the preacher at my small hometown Southern Baptist church. I can recall wondering how he seemed to read a part of his message, move away from the podium, and then come back to the place he left off. I wanted so much to be able to perform what seemed to me, at the time, an amazing feat. I was fascinated by preachers on television and would wake up early to watch them speak. I would dress up in a suit, go to my neighbor's house, and preach to them with my Bible in hand even before I could read. My grandmother, when she saw me screaming and kicking after my birth, said, "He's going to be a preacher." When I was just a small boy, I would crawl under the pew at church and lay face first on the floor when someone would pray.

In other words, I don't identify with people who don't know their purpose because I always seemed to know mine. I do identify with people who do not *follow* their purpose. For so many years, I'd run from being a preacher, and I'd tried everything until I finally accepted my call. I'd lived a life of bondage and separation from God. I can remember being so lost that I couldn't even stand hearing someone say the name Jesus around me. I was in rebellion from God and everything that had to do with Him. I would have rather spent my time drinking and partying than going after what seemed like a distant, unloving God.

Yet being a preacher isn't the prerequisite for operating in your calling. Your calling may not seem religious at all, though, in the end, when we follow God's design for our lives, it all falls under the divine and can be considered a calling. It's interesting to note that the word *vocation* comes from a Latin word meaning "to call." What you do for a living shouldn't be based on the benefit package or the starting salary. No, it should be based on what speaks to you. If you do what you love and love what you do, you'll never work another day in your life. Surprisingly, people who follow their passions stop chasing money and money starts chasing them (although generally not in the beginning). God throws His support behind what He's called His people to do.

> What you do for a living shouldn't be
> based on the benefit package or the starting salary.
> It should be based on what speaks to you.
> If you do what you love and love what you do,
> you'll never work another day in your life.

Have you felt as if you could never get ahead? Your account always seems to be in the negative before the next pay period. Your basic needs are met, but you still struggle to keep gas in the car and the lights on. This can come from things like poor budgeting, but more often than not, it's because we have made work an idol. It consumes all our time but never produces enough. It takes up our prayer time and devotion to God and keeps us from living a full life. If that's you, don't quit your job just yet, but know that it's time to start seeking God for something that calls to you—not just a source of income. Here's the story of how I learned my calling and started down the path to living a life of purpose.

My Journey to a Life of Purpose

I remember when it all changed for me. I'd been at a party at a friend's house, which was our usual hangout spot. I had been drinking, and I was about to smoke some weed with my friends. Just before I took a hit, it seemed as if time slowed down, almost to a standstill. I heard a voice in my spirit that I had never heard before. The voice said, "If you died tonight, where would you spend eternity?"

I snapped out of it and, in an attempt to get the voice out of my head, I immediately took a hit of marijuana. For the next few days, I experienced several strange moments like this one. I found myself turning the television to Christian shows. I was feeling something coming over me that I couldn't explain.

Little did I know that my cousin was a part of a prayer group, and they had been praying that I would be saved every night. Then it happened. I was working a night-shift job that I had taken to change the crowd I was hanging out with every night smoking weed and partying. Of course, taking the new job didn't stop me from doing what I had been doing before I fell right in with a new crowd. This was a strange crowd because they would party in the morning at 6 A.M. after their ten-hour shift instead of at night. So, I was getting off work and getting drunk and stoned at six in the morning.

One of those mornings, I got extremely drunk and very high. The friend I was with told me there were some girls at an apartment taking ecstasy. I had never tried this drug before, but I knew that people who were on it seemed to have a great time. So I got in the car with him and drove over as the sun was beaming in its early morning position. When we got to the apartment, I remember seeing these girls acting erratic and very strange. The person I was with took the drug, but I refused to take it. After a short time, I told him to take me home. He protested, but I told him that if he didn't take me home right then, I was going to beat him within an inch of his life. He believed me and drove me home. By this time, it was late in the morning, and I was drunk and high with only a few hours to try to get some sleep and sober up. I sank into my bed and, as the room spun out of control, I prayed the drunken man's prayer: "Lord, if you get me through this, I'll never drink again."

I woke up a few hours later, and I felt terrible. I could barely pull myself up out of the bed. I had to go to work because I was on a probationary period as a new employee and couldn't miss a day. As I languidly made my way to the shower, I wondered how I would be able to make it through this ten-hour shift before me. My head hurt, I was weak all over, and I felt as if I was going to vomit. My friend came to pick me up from work, and I struggled to make it to my first break.

At break, I went to the store and felt a little better. Back then, being a traditional Alabamian, I used smokeless tobacco—what we called "dippin'." I bought a can of dip and put some loose tobacco between my cheek and gum. When I walked into the warehouse, I felt something coming over me. It was as if my entire body was tingling. I felt as if I could really stop using tobacco if I wanted to. I took out the dip and went into the bathroom to wash my mouth out. As I did, I felt that same feeling I had when time seemed to stop at the party. I looked into the mirror and heard a voice, which I immediately recognized as God's. I was asked a question I'll never forget: "Is this who you want to be?"

I looked at myself and didn't like what I saw. I was an alcoholic, weed-smoking, angry, hurt person. I responded, "No, Lord, this is not who I want to be."

He responded, "Then give Me your life."

So I went through a list of things I wanted to change. I said to God that I never wanted to drink again in my life. I asked Him to take it from me, and I felt this surge of energy come over me. I knew that He had taken it away from me. Then I told Him I never wanted to cuss again. You have to understand that I cussed like a sailor back then, but I asked God to take it from me, and I felt it lift off of me. I asked Him to take the anger and the pain, and I could feel it leaving me. I asked Him to help me never to smoke weed, and I could feel it leaving me. I knew I was being completely transformed, so I gave up everything and asked Jesus to come into my heart and be my Savior. The one thing I held on to was sex. I told the Lord that I would stop cheating on my girlfriend and be faithful to her, but that was the one thing I wanted to keep in my life. As I went to the door and started to leave the bathroom with all those weights lifted off of me, I heard God again: "Why don't you give it all to me?"

I said, "Okay, Lord, I'll give you that as well." I left that bathroom completely changed. I began living my life completely sold out to God. I found my calling in the ability to communicate the transforming power I had experienced that faithful night, and it wasn't long until I accepted my calling to preach. I would like to tell you that after this point in my life, I never veered off the path again, but that's just not true. I lost my way several times, but God's loving and guiding hand has always put me back on course toward the vision He first gave me.

That being said, I know what it feels like to be off path and without direction, which is how you may be feeling now. It may be because you have yet to discover your purpose or, like me, you're not on the path to your purpose. I know what it's like to work a dead-end job and simultaneously feel dead on the inside. I know how it feels to want more out of life without being able to see beyond the next bill to even think about a dream. I also know how it feels to find purpose and get back on track. There's nothing in the world like living with passion and love for what you do. I remember working jobs that I couldn't stand. I recall Sunday nights being the worst time for me because I knew I had to get up the next morning and work a job that was sucking the life out of me.

I remember having to get up at 5 A.M. when I was in the army. I can see it now so clearly—walking out into the freezing cold mornings with snow and ice on the ground and my breath visible through the dark, frigid air. I would wear a thin jogging suit, gloves, and a beanie—which did nothing to keep the wind from cutting through my body like a knife. After an hour and a half of exercise, a quick shower, and breakfast, we were back on the job for another long day.

I learned a lot while in the military, but I couldn't wait to get out and pursue my calling. I had actually joined the military out of rebellion as a young preacher. I remember a season of being off my assignment as a preacher and thinking there was more in the world that I wanted to see. I became impatient with the process and thought about the quickest way to get out of Alabama with limited resources. I went down to the recruiter's office and signed up for the military. Soon after, I was on a plane for the first time to St. Louis. Then I went to training in San Antonio, with my first duty station in Germany, and finally made my last stop in Southern California.

I will never forget that first night of basic training. We arrived late and were processed as new recruits early in the morning with no sleep. We went to bed at 4 A.M. right before revelry woke the rest of the soldiers up at 4:30. I remember lying down on that bunk with a freshly shorn head and praying, "Lord, I got myself into this, and I ask You to be with me and help me get through it." Thankfully, He did just that. I had only myself to blame for my decision.

I still have dreams that I'm back in the military, and I wake up thanking God that it was just a dream. This is not a knock on those who have served twenty years or more, but I knew that it wasn't the thing I was put on earth to do.

When God released me from the army, I pursued ministry with all my heart! Of course, there were several jobs I had to work before I started in ministry, and although I was thankful for those opportunities to earn income, I always knew there was something more.

Finding Your Vision

As you read this book, I want you to consider if you are living your life on purpose. Do you love what you do? If not, then let's discover how to get on track. How do you get this place? It all begins with God.

Hebrews 12:2 declares that Jesus is *"the author and finisher of our faith."* Vision, if you haven't noticed by now, is your faith in God to perform His promises in your life. This not only covers biblical promises but also the personal promises in line with your vision. God will never tell you something that conflicts with His Word; it all will fit perfectly together. God's not going to call you to be something that will hurt you or other people. On the contrary, His calling for your life will bring out the best in you and in others. He will lead you on a path that is uplifting and will challenge you to become your highest self.

This, of course, takes an incredible amount of faith. Our faith begins when we trust in the author of faith, Jesus. Let's take a moment to consider faith. Faith doesn't mean that we always believe no matter what. You see, faith is a great risk that goes against nature; at times we will doubt if what we have faith for will ever come to pass. It's not natural to believe God—it's spiritual. So we go against what feels good on a natural level and must engage on the spiritual level, which takes a great amount of effort. Paul Tillich once said, "Doubt is not the opposite of faith; it is an element of faith."[2] He was describing the duality of faith. Real faith is when we get a vision so high that we doubt our ability to make it happen, which causes us to lean completely on God for its fulfilment. If we're going to live our lives to the fullest, we must do it by faith, even if it's a scary endeavor.

Faith in God to bring our vision to pass will always cause doubts and fears to arise. If we're not careful, our doubts will talk us out of our dreams. The key is to stay focused on our vision no matter what comes our way. All of this begins with God. Maybe you've heard people say to

2. Paul Tillich, *Systematic Theology*, vol. 2 (Chicago, IL: University of Chicago Press, 1957), 116.

put God first and then things will work out. This is not only a popular saying but a necessity as it relates to vision. Our vision originates with Him, and we must engage Him by faith to grasp the depth of what He has in store for us.

> Real faith is when we get a vision so high
> that we doubt our ability to make it happen,
> which causes us to lean completely on
> God for its fulfilment.

As I write about this topic, I'm thinking back again to my time in the military. I was working a good job as an instructor of EMT courses at the hospital. I had to get special permission to teach these courses from my normal unit. You see, I was a part of a tanker battalion, which was not the ideal job for a medic. I had been given this opportunity to work a cushy hospital job as a type of reward for my job performance at my old unit. As my time expired on the job at the hospital, I was set to go back to my unit. Around this time, my platoon leader at the hospital offered me another job. In the natural, I knew this would be impossible because they had already given me so much time away, but by faith, I believed God. I wrote down what I was believing for and put my faith on the line. Of course, doubt and unbelief tried to creep in, but I stayed focused on my vision.

The day came for the decision, and I was waiting for the phone call that would tell me whether or not I had the job. I ironed out my uniform for the hospital, put on my ID card, shined my boots, and prepared to go to work at the hospital. Sure enough, against all odds, I was approved to stay at the hospital. That, my friends, is the power of faith working through a vision. I prayed about it, wrote out my vision for the completion of it, and made faith moves as if I already had it. You, too, can tap into the power of faith and watch God move on your behalf. What you think about is what you will become—that's why it's important to get the right vision so you can center your thinking on the vision God has for your life.

> What you think about is what you will become—that's why it's important to get the right vision so you can center your thinking on the vision God has for your life.

God's vision for your life is always bigger than you can comprehend in your current state. That's the main function of a vision—to stretch you beyond your current belief system. So how do you get started on this fantastic vision? Let's look a Psalm 37:4 to help us find out. This verse says, *"Delight yourself in the LORD: and he shall give you the desires of your heart"* (AKJV). This is a lofty promise when taken at face value and can be potentially dangerous because most of us, when we get exactly what we'd thought we wanted, are left wanton and unfulfilled because it was what we wanted and not what He wanted for our lives.

We can see this example easily expressed in some of our relationship choices. Have you ever prayed that God would bless you with someone in your life? I'm talking about those times when your voice sounds a lot like God's voice, when your desire to connect with someone overrides your better judgement and drowns out God's voice. You feel a rush of emotions that always seems to come when you meet someone new who really makes an impression. This emotional rush is so strong that you forget the last time you felt that way, when the relationship ended in disaster. You blissfully go through the motions of praying about it because you just know that this is the one. Surely you wouldn't feel this way if he or she wasn't. You blindly connect with this person when all you had to do was pray about it and avoid future pain.

Then it happens, you get the person you so desired, only to wish you would have never asked for this person in the first place. It takes you months to untangle your life from this person. So, what happened? After the cocktail of chemicals in the brain wore off, you began to see his or her flaws. These flaws are hurtful and damaging to you and your future. So you try to back out as fast as you can without realizing how emotionally entangled you are with the wrong person. But, wait a minute, you got exactly what you wanted! Herein lies the dilemma with getting our desires. They are very rarely God's desires, and they leave us hurt, wounded, and in pain. One positive is that we are left with a lesson if we choose to heed the warning next time, praying about what we feel because what we feel isn't always God's will for our lives.

The original Hebrew of Psalm 37:4 shows us that this verse is better translated to mean that God will give us what *He* intended for us. This points us away from our own desires, which, as we have learned, can leave us heartbroken. The Bible is teaching us that we don't really know what we want and that we should seek what He wants for us. This seems logical when we isolate it and think of it rationally, but the heart can be very contentious when attempting to distinguish between our will and God's will. A popular adage is, "The heart wants what it wants." This is so true. It wants what it wants even when it's not good for us. That's why we have to weigh what our hearts want with what God wants. It may not appease you in the short term, but it will bring you a lifetime of fulfillment in the long run. I think the reason most people go after their desires and not God's desire for their life is because what we want seems to be better than what God wants. However, this is contrary to Scripture.

Because God is able to do more than we can ask or think, we should raise the level of what we ask or think.

Ephesians 3:20 says, *"Now unto him that is able to do exceeding abundantly above all that we ask or think…."* So what God has for us is beyond what we can conceive in our minds. Before you can conceive it and even articulate it, God has more on His mind. Not only is this encouraging as it relates to our desires, but it also shows just how capable God is in fulfilling His promises toward us. In fact, we can look at this another way—because God is able to do more than we can ask or think, we should raise the level of what we ask or think.

You see, God is going to do more, but we are setting the standard so low that when He does do something bigger, it doesn't seem so grand. Why? Because we are thinking and asking too little. The next time you ask God for something, or when you follow the steps of this book and write out your vision, take whatever you were going to write and amplify it. Ask for something even bigger. The one rule you'll be asked to abide by in this teaching is to always think big. The bigger you ask, the more God will be obligated to do more abundantly than you have asked or even thought. (See Ephesians 3:20.) That's why it's so important that your vision isn't written from a mental space but from your very soul. We need God to reveal to our spirit what great things He wants to do in our life and then conceive it in our minds. We must behold (as the title of this book proclaims) what He speaks to our hearts. When you capitulate to His will for your life, it will be beyond anything you could ever dream on your own. God knows exactly what it takes for you to be satisfied, exhilarated, and completely fulfilled!

> The one rule you'll be asked to abide by in this teaching is to always think big. The bigger you ask, the more God will be obligated to do more abundantly than you have asked or even thought.

You may ask, what's the first step? The first thing you have to do is develop a prayer life. Not the old, routine, religious prayer of your childhood but a thriving, life-changing prayer to God. When I was a child, I used to lie on my face under the pews whenever prayer would go forth in my small country church, but I didn't know why. I still lie on my face at times, and the most incredible moves of God in my life have occurred when doing so. I learned the principles and power of vision while lying on my face at my mother-in-law's house with nowhere else to turn. When I did this as a child, I didn't know this was a posture of respect; it just seemed appropriate back then. I knew prayer was important, but I didn't know how to do it properly or how to contact God. It took years of practice (and I'm still learning) to be able to access God through prayer. So this is not a time of meaningless words in attempt to punch the clock of prayer and say that you've performed your religious duty. On the contrary, this is a call to experience the awesome presence of the Creator—to talk to Him about His plan for your life. As Jeremiah 29:11 says, *"For I know the thoughts that I think toward you, saith the* Lord, *thoughts of peace, and not of evil, to give you an expected end."* I use the basic model of Philippians 4:6 in my approach to God. This verse says, *"Be anxious for nothing, but in everything by prayer and supplication…let your requests be made known to God"* (NASB).

I also know from the Old Testament that the main way God was approached was through the power of worship. Worship ushers in God's presence. Second Chronicles 5:13–14 says,

> It came even to pass, as the trumpeters and singers were as one, to make one sound to be heard in praising and thanking the Lord; and when they lifted up their voice with the trumpets and cymbals and instruments of musick, and praised the Lord, saying, For he is good; for his mercy endureth for ever: that then the house was filled with a cloud, even the house of the Lord; so that the priests could not stand to minister by reason of the cloud: for the glory of the Lord had filled the house of God.

We can deduct from this that we, too, can enter into God's presence when we make the sounds of worship and praise unto God in our hearts. And once we have His attention, we can bring our request before Him.

My Prayer Outline

I start my prayers out with worship and adoration. I try to keep "I" out of the first part of my prayers. True worship has everything to do with God and nothing to do with us. We will have an opportunity to deal with ourselves later in the prayer. This is a time reserved for Him as we entreat Him to experience His awesome presence. I have found that I've connected so deeply in worship that I forget what I was so worried about when I entered into prayer in the first place and feel as it has been taken care of through the power of His presence. My worship generally includes listening to worship music accompanied by going through God's attributes. I will tell Him things such as "You are wonderful," "You are excellent," "You are awesome," "There is none above You," "You are the King of Glory, Prince of Peace, Bright and Morning Star, magnificent, incredible, lovely, kind, and worthy of all honor and worship." When you can take the focus off yourself and put it completely on Him, you can slowly begin to feel His glory fill the room as it did in 2 Chronicles 5.

Next I go into confession. First John 1:9 says, *"If we confess our sins, he is faithful and just to forgive us our sins, and to cleanse us from all unrighteousness."* The next question should be, what is confession? I'm sure you've been like me and used a blanket prayer to cover all your sins. A popular way of doing this is saying, "Lord, I ask You to forgive me of all my sins." Hopefully you can see the fallacy in this prayer. This isn't confession at all. Confession requires a person to admit what they have done wrong. I've learned that confession is an extensive and sometimes arduous task. It involves the willingness to list and ask forgiveness for each individual sin. Only through actual confession can we experience true forgiveness. Many times, we are stuck in our lives because we have unrepented sins holding us back. This is not to condemn you but to show the blocks that are stopping the flow of God's awesome blessing in your life. So many times, the reason we pray the blanket prayer is because we do not intend to stop the behavior we're asking forgiveness for. We want forgiveness with no real change. Repentance involves confession and a turning away from the actions and behaviors that are causing a chasm between us and God.

After I've taken the time to repent and confess my faults, I start my time of supplication, or ask requests of God. I've learned that so many times we are in our heads trying to figure out how we are going to keep the lights on, pay our insurance, overcome a bad report from the doctor, and so many other cares of this life, when all we need to do is ask God for His help. That's why Paul tells us to be anxious for nothing. (See Philippians 4:6.) We have allowed anxiety to overtake us and get us so off track because we have stopped taking our cares to the One who holds the key to our peace. God has given us an open invitation to bring everything to Him. This is the actual place where vision is birthed. This is the time for you to ask God to show you what He wants for your life and boldly go into uncharted territory.

There are several examples in the Bible of men and woman doing extraordinary things simply by asking God to do more with their lives. None is perhaps greater than the story of Jabez. I would also like to juxtapose the story of Benjamin and Jabez because they both had the same name at their origin but had very different results in their lives. When Benjamin was born, his mother, Rachel, died giving birth to him. In her pain, she named him Benoni, which means "son of my sorrow and son of my pain." It's so imperative that you are careful what you call something when you're in pain. Right after her death, Rachel's husband stepped in and changed his name to Benjamin, which means "son of my right hand." This is a Hebrew idiom that means "son of my power." So God took his pain and turned it into his power.

The vision-writing process entails taking the pain of your past and turning it into the power that propels you into the future.

Someone reading this book needs to get that revelation. The vision-writing process entails taking the pain of your past and turning it into the power that propels you into the future. Benjamin got a name change so he wouldn't have to carry around this name as a sign of his mother's pain. Jabez's name had the same meaning—son of my sorrow or son of my pain. The difference is that Jabez's parents didn't die giving him this name; they did it on purpose. This man had to spend his entire life introducing himself as "pain." Jabez wasn't without options, however. He used the power of supplication to become something different than his name. In 1 Chronicles 4:10, we read his life-transforming prayer:

> *Jabez called on the God of Israel, saying, Oh that thou wouldest bless me indeed, and enlarge my coast, and that thine hand might be with me, and that thou wouldest keep me from evil, that it may not grieve me!*

God granted him that which he requested. Here we have a man who didn't have the luxury of a name change, but he got in contact with the life-changer. He asked God to make him the antithesis of what his name meant and to expand his territory that he may not cause pain. In essence, his family history and the labels that came with it no longer controlled his life. He decided that God was bigger than his circumstances and that he could have an expansive vision for his life that would be bigger than his name. The amazing thing is that God granted his request! Jabez isn't a special individual, he's just like you and me—only he dared to expand his vision and ask God to do the extraordinary in his life. That's what supplication is all about! It's taking the difficulties that life has thrown at you and seeking God to make something out of your life.

I want you to consider what you've been missing out on by neglecting your time with a vibrant, living God who wants nothing more than to see you enjoy life on all levels. He's waiting to change your routines, fire you up again, and bring back the vivaciousness you once enjoyed. It's not too late for you to get your life back on track!

Vision begins with a nexus between you and the divine. I want you to begin to seek God for your purpose. I want you to literally ask Him, "Lord, what do you want to do in my life? How do You want to express Yourself through me?" It's so exciting to find out your reason for being here. In fact, we all need you to fulfil your purpose because, ultimately, your purpose serves God and the people you will touch with your unique expression in the earth. God wants to ignite you with a fire that burns with passion for His desire for your life. The greatest life you could ever hope to live is one that brings Him glory.

Are you tired of going through the motions? Are you tired of just existing? Don't you want more out of life? There's a great big world out there, just waiting for you to be all you are called to be. It's time for you to find the place that I found on my mother-in-law's floor. I was so done with the way my life was turning out, and I decided to do something about it. I asked God, "What do You want to do with my life?" When He answered me, He transformed me forever. Is it always easy? Of course not! You will face challenges, you will experience loss and pain, but in the end, you will win if you don't quit. You may even want to put this book down right now and ask God, "What do You want to do through me?" Don't move until you hear Him. If you don't hear anything the first time you seek Him, don't give up. Keep seeking Him until you get answers. God wants to reveal your purpose to you because He put you here to do exactly what He created you for.

I believe the Bible reveals a clear path to God's presence in several Scriptures. As mentioned before, entering into God's presence is vital to the vision process. Here are some insights on how God communicates His vision for our lives through His manifest glory: Psalm 100:4 says to *"enter into his gates with thanksgiving, and into his courts with praise."* While studying the art of prayer, I did some investigation on the court of the Lord. One description about the Jewish court in *The New Unger's Bible Dictionary* reveals that it was called the place of the owl or the place of the ostrich. This seems insignificant until you delve into the unique ability of these two animals. The owl can see in the dark. When this is applied to a person entering the court or the presence of the Lord, we find out what the Hebrews meant when they called the court the place of the owl. When you enter God's presence, you become like an owl. Your vision opens, and you can see in the darkness shrouding your vision. In fact, you can see what other people may not be able to see.

When I was in the military, we had night vision goggles. These special goggles gave us the ability to see the enemy in the dark. As you spend time in God's presence, you your eyes will be opened to things that were there all the time but that you couldn't see—they were hidden to you. Once you engage God on a spiritual level through the power of prayer, a whole new world of possibilities opens to you. I've learned that every great vision comes under some type of attack, and that prayer allows us to see the enemy, even in the darkest of times. In seeing Him, you can engage Him the right way to secure the victory in your vision.

> I've learned that every great vision comes under some type of attack, and that prayer allows us to see the enemy, even in the darkest of times. In seeing Him, you can engage Him the right way to secure the victory in your vision.

Another interesting thing about an owl is its ability to turn its head around 360 degrees. Not only can this animal see in the dark, but it can also see everything around it at all times by rotating its head. Prayer is so vital because it gives us a view of all the things that could potentially try to stop our vision. It is so vitally important to see things when they are coming and be able to respond in a timely manner rather than having things hit us blindly from all sides. I'm sure we all know what it feels like to be blindsided by life. Prayer gives us the unique opportunity to prepare for whatever comes our way.

The place of the ostrich is just as informing about our time in God's spiritual court as the place of the owl. An ostrich is a flightless bird but is also the fastest bird, with running speeds of up to forty-three miles per hour. Just like the ostrich, through prayer, we can "run with the vision." (See Habakkuk 2:2.) The most interesting facet of this animal's abilities is not found in its attributes but in its attitude. It has often been said that a coward is like an ostrich that puts its head in the sand, but this is a common misnomer. Ostriches live in dessert plains and can see danger approaching from far off. It is said that when they see something coming, it looks as if they put their heads in the sand; actually, they hide their eggs and prepare to fight. When you spend time in God's presence, you, too, can see the enemy from far away, guard your vision, and prepare to defend your spiritual turf.

As we have discussed in this chapter, the first step in the vision process is allowing God to speak to your heart. If you haven't been a person of prayer or have become inconsistent in your prayers, this step may take a while. It takes time to open lines of communication and learn how to distinguish between your voice and God's voice. This seems as if it should be easy, but not when consider how God spoke to one of His greatest prophets. If anyone should have been able to hear clearly, it would have been the prophet Elijah. First Kings 19:11–12 reads,

> [The Lord] *said, Go forth, and stand upon the mount before the Lord. And, behold, the Lord passed by, and a great and strong wind rent the mountains, and brake in pieces the rocks before the Lord; but the Lord was not in the wind: and after the wind an earthquake; but the Lord was not in the earthquake: and after the earthquake a fire; but the Lord was not in the fire; and after the fire a still small voice.*

God wasn't in all the things we would have traditionally thought His voice would be in. The thunderous voice of the movies seems more fitting for the Lord, but many times He speaks in a still, small voice. Oh, how sweet it is to hear the whisper of God in your spirit. We must learn to clearly hear His voice and listen intently to His instructions. In them, we find the key to unlocking His desire for our lives.

Before we embark on this life-changing adventure with God, let's put first things first: Let's hear from the One who holds the keys to our future and wants nothing more than to release them to us. Take the time to seek Him and gain insight into your future. You will never be the same when you do this.

WHAT IS VISION?

THREE

WHAT IS VISION?

It's important that you know what vision is before you begin the vision process. One of the best ways to understand vision is to juxtapose natural vision with spiritual vision. These two types of vision mirror each other in so many ways. Both natural and spiritual vision involve the engagement of the mind to operate. Even the definition of the term *vision* contains natural and spiritual elements. Dictionary.com defines *vision* as:

1. The act or power of sensing with the eyes; sight.

2. The act or power of anticipating that which will or may come to be: prophetic vision; the vision of an entrepreneur.[3]

Natural vision is seeing what's before you by sensing with the eyes; spiritual vision is sensing what is to come on a supernatural level. Let's explore these two concepts even further.

Natural vision begins with the entrance of light. It's amazing to note that natural vision has very little to do with the eyes and more to do with the mind. Your eyes act primarily as light receptors, but it's your brain that interprets what is seen. About 30 percent of the brain is used in processing vision—this is significantly more than any of the other

---

3. "vision," *Dictionary.com*, http://www.dictionary.com/browse/vision?s=t.

senses. Vision, then, is more of a mental process than a function of the eyes. In fact, Hermann von Helmholtz, a German physician and physicist, studied the brain's function as it relates to vision, and found that it's primarily based on preconceived notions. This simply means that the mind associates what it has learned with what it sees—so even if an image in the mind is wrong, the eyes will process it the way it's been taught to perceive it.

A person raised in a racially charged environment will look at certain ethnicities and see an enemy or someone to be feared. I have personal experience with this. My mother and grandmother never spoke in a negative or derogatory way about another person of a different ethnic origin around me. The first time I heard the "n-word" was when my stepfather moved in. He used many racial overtones and epithets when he moved into my house. This is one habit I never seemed to pick up in my life. I was always fascinated by other cultures and was influenced by Run-D.M.C., LL Cool J, and the Fat Boys; to me, Black people were the coolest people I had ever seen. Not to mention, I was tremendously influenced by Prince and Michael Jackson, whose music was the soundtrack of my childhood in the 1980s. Taking this all into account, you have to realize that I was no aficionado on race relations living on the outskirts of Birmingham, Alabama. Most of this was a no-brainer in the sense that my path never crossed that of another Black person. Out of thousands of people who went to my high school, there were maybe twenty Black people, and they seemed to fit in with us. This was, of course, out of necessity, grouped in with a majority of White people. We played sports with them, and after that, we left them alone and they left us alone. Regrettably, this was the area and time that I grew up in. I heard a lot of racial slurs from my stepfather, and I was pretty much immune to it. When I befriended a Black student in the ninth grade, he told me, "You can be friends with him at school, but he's not coming in this house." I remember thinking how stupid that was and wanted to challenge his resolve on that rule, but I didn't want to subject my friend to that. I did, however, think that most White men his age thought this way—and that was a way to connect on a deeper level with men I wanted to seek approval from as a young man.

Thankfully, I had an uncle who changed that line of thinking in me. This had become a preconceived notion born from my home environment. I was staying with my cousin in Auburn, a few hours outside of Birmingham, as I did every Sunday. While the three of us were riding down the road, I saw a Black man walking down the street and used the "n-word." I did it thinking it would get a favorable result from this Southern White man. Instead, my uncle pulled over on the side of the road and scolded me. He told me that that word was the wrong way to address a Black person and that as long as I was in his house, I was not allowed to use that word. That one moment began to shatter my paradigm. I saw a White man living in a rural area, even more far removed from Black people than my town, refusing to accept that as proper vernacular. My preconceived notion was shifted.

Even old racists can change their ways. If you remember the story of when I received Christ, you will recall that the first person I'd encountered after my experience was a Black man. His name was Rodney Herring, and he remains a friend to this day. It's amazing because he has such an incredible, laid-back demeanor and an understanding of how to connect with people regardless of race. I tell you that because he won over my dad. It blows my mind how much my dad fell in love with Rodney. After all these years, they still keep in contact. I can even recall my stepfather calling Rodney his son! That's something he never called me! Rodney was the beginning of his walls coming down, but I have to say, my interracial children have also had a significant impact on him. His ideologies were shattered when he encountered how much those children love him. They caused him to change his entire way of thinking, especially as it relates to interracial children.

If that wasn't enough, he had a near-death experience in which he was lying dead on an operating room table. During this time, he was ushered into a beautiful garden made out of marble, and it was full of roses. A man approached him in a robe, but he couldn't see his face. The man spoke to him and said, "Your time is not up yet; I still have something left for you to do." When my stepfather told me this story, I saw him do something I had never seen him do before—he cried. I can't recall last time he used a racial slur or said anything negative about a person of another race. I have seen how his preconceived notions have changed. This is coming from a man that came up during the Civil Rights Movement with all the hate that poured out of Birmingham. He was in the middle of that mind-set that so opposed the rights of African Americans in the United States. Yet with all of that history and hatred, he was able to change the way he thought. If he can do it, anyone can!

I think it's important to take the time to get personal about preconceived notions, and racism is a perfect conduit for that. Growing up where and when I did, I heard that all people were God's children but that Blacks and Whites didn't mix. My stepfather had not believed in equality; under no circumstances were people from other races supposed to mix. I grew up with this belief and carried it with me even when I got saved. I will never forget the day God spoke to my heart and told me to leave my church and join a 3,000-member Black church. He told me that this was not some kind of mission trip but that I was to completely give my entire life to Him serving in that ministry. I, of course, had a steep learning curve, both on a cultural level and on a worship-style level. Plus, I would be submitting to the leadership of a Black pastor. All these concepts made people around me question if I was losing my mind. Why would I, a nineteen-year-old White kid with his entire life before him, do something like that? They couldn't hear what I was hearing or see what I was seeing.

Even thought I was so completely sure about my decision, I still had one caveat. I told God very plainly that I would join this church and give it my all but that I would not, under any circumstance, marry a Black woman. This was non-negotiable to me. Now why in the world would I say something like that? It had been drilled into my head that White and Black people could be friends but that they couldn't, under any circumstance, comingle in marriage. I was also given a misinterpretation of Bible verses to back up this racist point of view. It didn't take me long to find beauty in another race. In fact, I saw the most beautiful, intelligent, strong, loving women I had ever encountered. Needless to say I am now married to a beautiful African American woman who has given me four incredible children. What happened? Being exposed to an environment that was different than mine allowed me to begin to question all my social norms and cultural constructs that had blocked me from seeing that all people are equal on all levels. I went from projecting a thought given to me to completely changing what I saw and, therefore, changing my preconceived notion. I learned to think differently, and those thoughts changed what I saw with my eyes. This is the power of the mind's neuroplasticity and its ability to change even the most inculcated thoughts.

The only way to change a person's vision is to change his or her preset way of thinking. I admit that this is a daunting task because most people who have preconceived notions aren't aware of them. I have made the mistake of pointing out someone's overtly racial views, only to be reprimanded with, "I'm not a racist; why, my best friend is Black." Until this person, by way of life events or outside information, begins to challenge his views instead of hide them in the comfort of people who agree and solidify those beliefs, he will remain captive to the powers of perception, even if that perception is wrong. The same thing happens in spiritual vision. If we were raised in an economically depressed environment, then we will automatically register with that mind-set, even if God wants to show us something different. A new spiritual possibility becomes difficult to see because we have been trained to see something else.

I know I have struggled with this concept, because I grew up in a house where we never seemed to have enough money. My family did the best they could, and I always had something to eat. Food may have come from a dent store, or had a black and white label on it, but I ate. Yes, the power was turned off at times, but for the most part, it was on. However, there was always this feeling that there was never enough to go around. Lack became engrained in my mind-set. I grew up with a scarcity mentality. It took some serious soul work to understand that God was a provider and that He was a God of more than enough. I also had to get a vision of what abundance looked like and see that vision through as an experiential example rather than just a theory.

> Lack became engrained in my mind-set. I grew up with a scarcity mentality. It took some serious soul work to understand that God was a provider and that He was a God of more than enough.

Even the Bible deals with the power of perception, and perhaps there is no greater example of this than Psalm 92:10, which reads, *"But my horn shalt thou exalt like the horn of a unicorn: I shall be anointed with fresh oil."* This verse seems innocent enough, and the concept seems to be straightforward. You have a unicorn and some oil. Got it. It's not until you consider the unicorn that its meaning becomes clear. Of course, a unicorn is a mythological being and doesn't exist. This can be dismissed as a simple metaphor, but there's more to it. When this verse was written, the translators didn't have a word to describe the animal they saw. Modern translations properly refer to this animal as a wild ox. So why were the early translators so baffled? The reason is because the only thing they had to decipher this animal was a Babylonian pictogram—a picture sent to someone as correspondence. The animal depicted in the picture was supposed to be a wild ox, which has two horns, but the picture presented a profile view. An animal with two horns appeared to only have one, thus the mistranslation. This is exactly what happens when we look at a person who has seen his or her vision come to pass or has been tremendously successful. Generally, people look at only one side of the story. They don't see the sacrifice, the pain, or the struggle that went into the fulfillment of that vision. People completely mistranslate how a person got where he or she is in life. Their perception causes them to miss the reality of the process for promise. That's why it's so important to deal with your misperceptions so you can shape a new way of thinking and see God's hand working in your vision.

Another way natural and spiritual vision correlate is found in what the eyes actually see. Natural vision involves two eyes and two retinas. The retina is a layer at the back of the eyeball containing cells that are sensitive to light and that trigger nerve impulses that pass via the optic nerve to the brain, where visual image is formed. We all see two images. Every person has double vision. One of the ways this is rectified is through the corpus callosum. This is the matter that lies between the two hemispheres of the brain and has, as one of its main functions, the ability to take two images and merge them into one. Similarly, when we activate our vision from a spiritual perspective, we also encounter double vision. We have the image that God is projecting in our spirit and the old patterns that are stubbornly implanted in our current way of thinking. This is why so many have dreamed but have given up, simply because the previous way of thinking cast such a long shadow, with too many doubts to overcome.

> There always seems to be a great challenge in the beginning of your dream that causes you to look at the duality of your situation. Yes, you are believing to work at your dream job, but your current job environment is becoming more and more difficult to manage. This is the push-pull of a dream that we all must face.

Perhaps you have experienced double vision when attempting to dream in the past. I know that I have been sick and found myself preaching on healing. Why? Because I recognized my double vision. An experience in my current state didn't line up with my future state, so instead of focusing on what I didn't want, that is, my sickness, I focused on what I did want, my healing. I have seen my life go directly opposite of my vision. In fact, that's how it normally works. There always seems to be a great challenge in the beginning of your dream that causes you to look at the duality of your situation. Yes, you are believing to work at your dream job, but your current job environment is becoming more and more difficult to manage. This is the push-pull of a dream that we all must face. If things remained comfortable, we would never dream for something better. We would be satisfied with living a calm, lackluster life. Sometimes it takes a little chaos to get us moving in the right direction.

Albert Einstein once said, "Nothing happens until something moves."[4] Interestingly enough, magnets are used quite frequently in movement of mechanics. We think of our life as we think of magnets: in the sense of negative and positive. If I only get the positive, I will feel really good about myself, but I'll never move. It takes some negativity to mix with the positive to start the movement process. So don't fret when you're faced with double vision, because it's a necessary part of your forward progress. You will see a battle in your finances when you start believing God for more abundance in your life. You will get cravings for food that you've never had before when you decide to start eating right and become more health conscious. You will see the old ways of thinking attempting to drag you down. This is all to be expected, but with focus and determination, you cannot be denied.

Just as the brain uses the corpus callosum to bring two images together into one in natural vision, so we need a spiritual corpus callosum to regulate the image of unsuccessfulness and merge it with the possibility of success to change outcomes in our lives. We eradicate double vision when the new vision becomes more believable and achievable than the old vision. This can take some time. We have to commit to renewing our minds. This is done in the repetition of speaking our dreams through positive confessions. It's important to note that even before you have developed a vision, you can start retraining your mind through the Word of God. Romans 12:2 says, *"Be not conformed to this world: but be ye transformed by the renewing of your mind."* True transformation is just like natural vision: it's as much of a mental exercise as it is a spiritual one. You can literally use God's Word to change your brain's way of thinking. The brain has neuroplasticity, which means it

---

4. Albert Einstein quoted in Robert J. Ringer, *Action: Nothing Happens until Something Moves* (Lanham, MD: M. Evans, 2004), 14.

is malleable and can bend toward whatever influence is exerted over it. That's why what you think and what you say are so important.

> True transformation is just like natural vision: it's as much of a mental exercise as it is a spiritual one. You can literally use God's Word to change your brain's way of thinking.

The Bible tells us, *"Finally, brethren, whatsoever things are true, whatsoever things are honest, whatsoever things are just, whatsoever things are pure, whatsoever things are lovely, whatsoever things are of good report; if there be any virtue, and if there be any praise, think on these things"* (Philippians 4:8). This is a blueprint on how to govern your thought life. What you think is so vitally important because it becomes what you say, and what you say is ultimately what you will become. Proverbs 18:21 says, *"Death and life are in the power of the tongue: and they that love it shall eat the fruit thereof."* You have the power to create a life or death situation by what you say. That's why it's important to use God's Word as your word. Hebrews 4:12 states that God's Word is *"sharper than any twoedged sword."* The word *"twoedged"* is translated from the Greek word *distomos* and means "two mouths." God speaks His Word out of His mouth, which is the first mouth. Then you speak what He has said about you out of your mouth, the second mouth.

We have to combat what we are currently experiencing in our life with what we believe is going to happen. We overcome double vision created in our life when we dare to dream by what we focus on. For example, you may be dealing with debt that seems to be swallowing you up and consuming your thought life. Of course, this is a present reality and needs to be remedied, and that's why it stays at the forefront of your mind. Perhaps you have written your vision for debt freedom, but the debt is still there. What do you do to deal with the double vision?

Find all the Scriptures you can on debt freedom and speak them until they impregnate your every thought and action. Quote verses such as Deuteronomy 28:12 and 15:6, which both say that we shall lend to many nations but we shall not borrow. Claim those Scriptures for yourself and personalize them. You may say something to the effect of, "Father, in the name of Jesus, I am now succeeding at being a lender and not a borrower." If you consistently train your mind with the power of God's Word and solidify those thoughts with words, you'll see a powerful transformation in your life. Then you will no longer have double vision, but God's Word will become the corpus callosum that will transform the negative into the positive and will produce forward progress.

> If you consistently train your mind with the power of God's Word and solidify those thoughts with words, you'll see a powerful transformation in your life.

The interesting thing about vision is not only it is primarily a mental exercise, based on preconceived notions, or that it creates double vision, but that when the image from the mind is projected onto the retinas, which are also known as the movie screen of the eyes, we see something interesting in the images—the image is inverted. Not only do we have double vision, but we also see upside down. The optical part of the brain takes the upside-down images and turns them right-side up.

This is also true in spiritual vision. I have never received a vision in my life with all of the elements present. In fact, it's always been the opposite. I remember when God spoke to me to leave the comfort of the Southern Baptist church of my childhood in the rural confines of my small town of Clay, Alabama. You see, when I had been saved at my job, I had come out of that bathroom a changed man. The first person I encountered was a Black man who worked with me. He and I hadn't spoken very much and, quite frankly, I thought he was Muslim because everyone called him Malcom X and he was always talking about God. I figured that, if he was a Black Muslim, then he wasn't trying to convert me, and that I should just leave him alone. When I emerged from that bathroom a changed man, he looked right at me and, sensing something, said, "Man, you just got saved." He pulled me to the back of the warehouse and immediately began to minister to me. After some time of impartation, he said, "Hey, we have a tent revival going on at my church this week; you should come with me." Without hesitation, I said yes.

Little did I know that I was being invited to a church that boasted a membership of three thousand, and no one there was White. I stumbled into a Black Pentecostal tent revival and saw things that never happen in my country Baptist church. I immediately fell in love with the passion in the praise and in the preaching. Soon after, I joined this congregation and started a new path on the road to my destiny. I remember how my friends responded to this move. They all thought I was crazy for joining this Black church in the heart of the inner city. I had several family members and friends turn their back on me.

I had been given a vision, and I couldn't find any friends to help me. My friends were upside down. Thankfully, God surrounded me with a new family and new friends who saw God's hand on me and supported my vision. This caused what was upside down to turn right-side up.

I've never had enough money to make a vision happen when first presented. That's because God always challenges me to dream beyond my resources. I remember when I first started marketing my ministry. I was working for a church, but I had limited recourses and no one to help with getting my ministry out there. One of the first things I did was stay up all night teaching myself how to upload videos to YouTube. This was no easy task for someone who was completely computer illiterate, but I was determined to get the message God had given me out into the world. I couldn't afford to hire someone to do it, so I taught myself how. Back then, the most popular social media platform was Myspace, so I used that to my advantage. I posted my YouTube links on everyone's pages. I stayed up for hours posting to people's pages to get the message out. My pastor, who was a bishop, gave me a book with all the bishops' emails in the Church of God in Christ. emailed a link of one of my videos to all the bishops. Months later, I stood on stage at the Holy

Convocation for the Church of God in Christ, and all the bishops had come in right before I had to speak. One of the bishops told me that they had all come in early to hear me. What propelled me into this defining moment? Not accepting that my lack of money could stop me from promoting my ministry. My money was upside down, but my vision turned it right-side up.

Perhaps you can relate to this in your own life. Do you feel as if there are so many things you want to do with your life, but you can't see it happening because you don't have enough money? It's imperative for you to understand that you will never have enough money. God wants to do something in your life that your current financial status can't support. That's the whole message of the need for vision. It goes beyond your natural ability. Upside down seems to be standard procedure as it relates to the alpha stage of a vision, yet God has a way of using vision to turn the upside-down images and circumstances in your life right-side up. Anticipate that things will be upside down when you begin to unleash the vision God has given you for your life. You will quickly learn that if you stick with it, it will always turn around in your favor!

> God wants to do something in your life that your current financial status can't support. That's the whole message of the need for vision. It goes beyond your natural ability.

Vision is not only the ability to sense with the natural eyes but the ability to perceive through divine revelation what's about to happen in your future. God wants to give you insight into the great things He's about to show you, and I want to show you how to harness this power and watch it come to pass in your life. You will have to eradicate preconceived notions because what you see will be greater than what you have ever experienced in your past. Your old vision for your life will stand in stark contrast to your new vision and will create temporary double vision. Thankfully, your new vision can merge them together and cause you to see what's to come instead of what's been. Yes, you will see upside down. In certain situations and circumstances, it will look as if your vision will never turn right-side up. If you stay with the process, it will work! Are you ready? We know how to get a vision and what vision is, so now it's time to find out how to write our vision. Let's go!

DREAM BIG

FOUR

DREAM BIG

The best thing to remember when starting on your vision is to go big. That's right, this isn't the time to limit your imagination; it's the time to go for it all. You have all green lights at this point in the process. You have to get your mind to a place where you see more than what's in front of you. God is big, abundant, and incredible, and He wants to share all this with you. Just imagine that you have such abundance that you can provide more than enough for yourself and for your family. You can go on vacation to that exotic land or live in a house that's suitable for you and your family. You can enjoy a fulfilling job or own your own business and actually love what you do. Guess what, you can have it all. God loves you, and He doesn't want to see you struggle to make it.

I know what it's like to feel stuck and wonder how you're going to make it to the end of the week let alone dream for something big. I know what it's like to scrape the change out of the ashtray to pay for enough gas to get home from work. I also know what it's like to take a step back and think about what it would be like to live differently. Sometimes that's all it takes—taking the time to allow yourself to daydream, to envision something better in your life, to put pen to paper, and to express what you see. In the past, I removed myself from my current situation and projected myself into the future, asking myself what it would look like if everything worked out perfectly. I want you to sit back, quiet your mind, and think about what your life could become. Let's begin by asking some simple questions.

Envisioning Your Relationship with God

If everything worked out perfectly and you could become all that God has placed before you in your vision, what would you see? Write it on a piece of paper or type it on your tablet, computer, or phone. Let's start this awesome journey.

> Perhaps the most important thing you can do as it relates to vision is to not complain about what you're currently getting and to ask yourself, *What do I want?*

The first question I want you to ask yourself as we begin is this: What does your relationship with God look like? I always start here because I know that vision begins with Him; it's important that we put Him first. Before we go any further, you may find it helpful to consider what you don't want. This may be your current place with God. Then ask yourself what you do want. Perhaps the most important thing you can do as it relates to vision is to not complain about what you're currently getting and to ask yourself, *What do I want?* How is your relationship with your Creator now? Do you feel disconnected? If so, write out what being connected would look like. You may write something like, "I feel God's presence when I pray and when He talks to me." Has your relationship with Him become stagnant? Then you could write out in detail how you see your connection with Him being alive, passionate, and fulfilling. You may write that every day is a new adventure with God and that you are stimulated by your nexus with Him. What do you want your connection with God to be like? Do you want to see mysteries in the ancient Scriptures that illuminate your path? Do you want to feel the pure ecstasy of His presence? Do you want to feel the peace that passes all understanding? (See Philippians 4:7.) Write out how you see yourself as if you are already there. Here's an example: "I feel completely connected to God, and I feel His love surrounding me every day. I trust Him because I can see and feel His power working in my life." I want you to write as if you were already there, because that's how faith works. You have to see it, feel it, and be it as if you already had it.

I recently wrote out a new vision for my life and focused on my relationship with God. I paid particular attention to things I wanted to change about myself and how I could become more like Him. This part of my vision has led me to discover deep-seated wounds that I had never consciously paid attention to. I was going forward with my life but had failed to deal with some pain from my childhood. It wasn't until I engaged God on this deeper level that I discovered these wounds. I realized that I was carrying a lot of unforgiveness in my heart toward my mother and my stepfather. When my mother married my stepfather, he was kind and friendly, but soon after the marriage, he became cold and angry toward me. I soon realized that I was the baggage to the relationship and that he wanted to get rid of me. The less time he could spend with me, the better. He obviously wasn't ready to take on a son, especially one that wasn't his.

My mother seemed to do nothing in response to his actions, which caused resentment to build up in me over time. I didn't realize that I was glossing over this pain and carrying unforgiveness in my heart toward both of them. When I asked God to allow my private relationship with Him to bleed into my personal life, I started seeing this problem on display. Through my deepened level of connection to Him, I was able to experience healing in the areas I needed it most. That's why it's so important to ask this question first, because there could be something lurking in your heart that could stop your progress. So are you ready for a deeper walk with the Lord? If so, picture what your connection to Him looks like and strengthen the bond that's the origin of all your dreams.

Here is an excerpt of what I recently wrote about my relationship with God in my vision:

I am now close to my Lord and Savior, Jesus Christ. I feel His presence every day when I pray. I seek Him on a daily basis. I have a fulfilling, growing relationship with Him. What He shares with me in my intimate times with Him is revealed in my everyday life.

As you can see, my vision is heavy on connection and translation into my everyday life. This is what I picture when I think of a real connection with God. It's more than just something I do; it affects my entire life. I want my relationship with Him to be present in my roles as a husband, father, friend, and person. I want to become more like Him by seeking Him with my whole heart. I want you to picture what your ideal relationship with God would look like and to write it down. At the top of the page, write "vision." I also like to write the date so I can look back on it and compare when it actually comes to pass. Next, I want you to title a paragraph "God." Under that, I want you to write in detail what a satisfying relationship with God looks like to you.

Envisioning Your Family Life

Title the next paragraph "family." This is the space allotted for you to describe what your family life would look like if you could have a great connection with your spouse, child(ren), mother, father, or any other family member. So many people are dealing with marital problems. This can be expected because two people are trying to become one. Each brings his or her own emotional baggage to the situation. Each person projects onto the other expectations birthed out of life experiences that date back to childhood and to his or her first boyfriend or girlfriend. Expectations always run high when two people meet and the love potion kicks in. However, endorphin levels settle, and we have to meet the real person behind the projected sense of self-worth. Not only do we have to deal with the other person but we have to deal with ourselves. Relationships really have very little to do with the other person and more to do with ourselves. How do we attempt to know another person when we know so little about ourselves? Relationships are difficult and challenge us on the deepest levels. Therefore, it's important that we make it a part of the vision process. Ask yourself these questions: What does my ideal marriage look like? How is my connection with my spouse, child(ren), and parents? What can I do to improve my most intimate relationships? If I did those things, what would that look like? Write it out in detail leaving nothing out. Here's an example of a portion of my family vision: "My marriage is healthy and supportive and filled with passion and love. My children are happy, they always feel loved and supported, and we teach them the ways of the Lord." Think about what your marriage looks like and write it down. Think about your kids and how you want them to turn out and write that out. Powerful things happen when you write a vision for your family.

Envisioning Your Career

Next, I want you to write out what your ideal job or business looks like. If you could do anything, what would that be? If you suddenly had all the money you could ever want or need, what would you do with your life? What would you dedicate yourself to? If money wasn't the driving force behind your employment, what would you do? This is how I want you to approach this part of the vision. You see, you have only one life to live. Why not live it on purpose? Why not make the days count instead of let them pass you by? God wants you to live your days in service to Him. One of the main ways we do this is through work. Most of us spend more time at work than anywhere else. Why not spend that time doing what you love and what brings glory to God? Writing your vision frees you to look into the future and imagine what this looks like for you. Maybe you dream of owning your own restaurant; starting a new technology company; being a doctor, writer, pastor, speaker, missionary, or builder—whatever it is, you can do it! The first step in seeing this part of your vision is being bold enough to dream it, see it, speak it, and plan for its success—then do it!

The first step in seeing this part of your vision is being bold enough to dream it, see it, speak it, and plan for its success—then do it!

When I first wrote my vision, I knew exactly what I wanted to do. I wanted to travel the world preaching and inspiring people with what God had given me. I saw myself traveling to the largest cities in America and around the world, speaking in the largest churches and at the largest conferences. I wasn't afraid to dream the dream again. Back then, I saw myself standing in front of thousands at the aforementioned Holy Convocation for the Church of God in Christ and preaching. I saw myself flying from city to city to speak in front of thousands. I knew my calling; I just didn't know how to draw a connecting line between where I was and where I wanted to be. Vision became the tool I employed to reach my goal. You, too, can use the power of a written vision to do exactly what you feel called to do.

My advice to anyone is to follow his or her passion. That's the key to unlocking happiness and wealth in life. When I wrote out my vision for my ideal job, it looked something like this: "I am preaching around the world. I am flying from city to city spreading the message of hope that God has given me. I am preaching in the Holy Convocation for the Church of God in Christ." I made a choice that day that my life would somehow, someway, become what I saw in my mind.

You, too, can make this choice to throw away the shackles of just existing and thrive in a field that adds value to your life and supports you in every way. It doesn't matter your age. You're never too young or too old to dream of the perfect job. It does exist. It begins in your spirit, translates to your mind, and then manifests in your life. Whatever you give your time and attention to will be what you have. Whatever you expend cerebral energy on will eventually be produced in your life. Write out in detail what you desire to be, and it will happen if you continue to follow the steps of the vision process.

Envisioning Your Finances

Next, focus on the one thing people try to be the most discreet about—how much money they want to make. For some reason, especially in the church, we struggle with not having enough money, but we don't involve God in that part of our lives. So many people are afraid that when they talk about money in church, they are preaching prosperity. The funny thing is that God has promised us in so many Scriptures that He wants to prosper us.

The Lord will command the blessing on you.
(Deuteronomy 28:8 esv)

Beloved, I wish above all things that you may prosper.
(3 John 2 akjv)

This book of the law shall not depart from your mouth, but you shall meditate on it day and night, so that you may be careful to do according to all that is written in it; for then you will make your way prosperous, and then you will have success. (Joshua 1:8 nasb)

These are just a few examples of verses that contain the subject of prosperity. There are many more that deal with abundance, needs being met, and debt freedom. The point is that God is concerned about every aspect of your life, including your finances.

I remember the first time I was faced with the question of how much money I would like to make, and I shot the number extremely small. This was because, in my mind, my past lack was larger than my future prosperity. However, I knew that I could dream big and that I would meet milestones along the path to that dream. I was willing to dream. I haven't reached my original number yet, but I'm working on it. Every year I come closer and closer, but where I am is nowhere near where I was when I wrote out my original vision. I want you to pick a number. Don't worry about how big it is now (we are going to work with some reasonable numbers soon), but for now, if you could have any amount of money, what would it be? Is it a million dollars? Maybe one hundred million dollars? I know this sounds crazy, but this isn't the time to limit yourself. I read somewhere that you should double the number for how much you want to make in a year, because we all have the propensity to think smaller than we should. Maybe you don't feel comfortable going for the big number, and you just want to go for making more money next year. Well, what would that look like? When you get that number, I want you to double it! After you reach that goal, I want you to start thinking even bigger. Just like for anything else in life, you need to have a vision for your money. We all need more money, and most of us never seem to have enough. What if you could change all of that? What if, through the power of vision, you could move from barely enough to more than enough? You can have it all—a great home life, a connection to God, and more than enough money to enjoy your life without constant worry about what the future holds.

Envisioning Your Environment

The next step in this process is to think about where you live. If you could live anywhere, in any type of house, what would it look like? I believe environment is so important. If you don't believe me, then look at the rate of kids that graduate when placed in great schools with great teachers as opposed to underfunded schools with teachers who don't care. When I lived in Alabama, I went to a county school that was recognized as a Blue Ribbon school. If you graduated from my school with a lower GPA than someone who graduated from a non-Blue Ribbon school, your grades were still considered to be better based on the high standards for academia at my school. It wasn't until I started mentoring in a city school that I saw the disparaging difference in standards. I remember the teachers telling me I could speak to their kids as long as I liked. The reason was simple—that was less time they had to do their job. It seemed as if the teachers were there for one reason and one reason only—they needed a job. There was no passion to shape a future generation, no drive, no care, no concern. It was disheartening, to say the least. I saw something different in those kids. I saw dreams and aspirations, but they didn't have a mechanism by which to pull themselves out. So I did what I knew best to do. I taught them how to write out a vision for their lives. I wanted to see these kids defy the odds and succeed regardless of their environment.

> Vision is all about breaking the natural order of things to supernaturally bring to pass the vision for your life.

In addition, your environment is important as it relates to your future. You can change your environment and live in the house of your dreams in the perfect setting. I want you to take out the same sheet of paper and write out in detail what your house looks like and where it is. This part of the process is particularly dear to my heart because I wrote myself into a million-dollar home the same year that I was homeless. I know the power of vision when it comes to a home, because I had it work out exactly as I had written it down. It didn't come the way I thought; that's what vision is all about—breaking the natural order of things to supernaturally bring to pass the vision for your life. This is where you want to write down your dream house. If you could live anywhere and in the perfect house, where and what would that be? Make sure you write all the details so you can attract exactly what you desire. My first vision looked something like this: "I am moving into a beautiful three-story house over the mountain. I have a pool, a multiple-car garage, Viking stoves, a Jacuzzi, and mountain views. I have a circular driveway and a manicured lawn. My house is worth a million dollars." That's just a portion of what I wrote. Now dream of the most beautiful house in the perfect location.

Envisioning Your Health

This is an area that so many of us neglect, yet it's one of the greatest investments you can make into your future self. It doesn't matter where you live or how much money you have if you don't have your health. When I wrote out my vision the first time, I weighed 245 pounds and was overweight. I was in my thirties, but I had high cholesterol and needed to get my health under control. I wrote out a vision for my weight and health. In one year, I went from 245 to 180 pounds. I'll never forget how big I was when I stood on the stage at the convocation. When I saw myself on a DVD, I knew I had to do something. My goal was to get my weight down to 180 pounds before the next convocation. It just so happens that I was invited back to speak again, and the week that I flew out to St. Louis, I stepped on the scale and had reached my goal. Was this just a magical thing because I wrote out a vision for my weight-loss goals? The answer, of course, is no.

As we progress through this process, I'll teach you how to write out a strategy for your goals so you can have something to actively do in the process. Just know that it all starts with writing out what you want to look and feel like. I want you to write your dream for your health now. You may be facing a heath challenge, and that's okay. You can write out what healing looks like for you. You may want to lose some weight—that's an obtainable dream as well. What do you see in this area? Write it out in detail, and begin the journey to a better you today. God wants you to look great, feel great, and live a healthy life that you can enjoy for years to come.

Envisioning Your Emotional Health

Write out what your life looks like from an emotional standpoint. So many of us have been deeply wounded in our childhoods and have never recovered. Many of us have been caught up in addictive behaviors that have affected us on an emotional level. It's time that we become introspective. I have found that most people who live emotionally stunted lives are afraid to face themselves. They're afraid to deal with things that have damaged them in the past. We are so prone to trying to suppress emotional wounds, but this comes at a very heavy price. When we bury and compartmentalize our pain, it finds a way out. It spills out into our mental and emotional health. So many times, we take it out on ourselves. There are so many who are depressed, and they don't know why. The reason is because of their unresolved issues. They are lurking beneath the conscious level, dictating and defining them every day.

We also externalize emotional traumas, taking them out on those around us—generally, the ones closest to us. Unresolved issues from our childhood or bad relationships can shape the way we see the world. We may have never recovered. They may have caused us more harm than if we would have just faced them. Admittedly, it is very difficult to face the darker sides of ourselves. We would rather ignore those painful areas, but they manifest themselves whether we acknowledge them or not. Here's a portion of my own personal pain that I had to face and deal with to recover my emotional sanity and finally come to a place of peace.

It was probably around the age of four or five that I began to notice something different about my family. I didn't have a father in the home, and I began to ask questions about who he was. I was told that my dad was the man that my mom was previously married to. She told me that he was my father and that he didn't want anything to with me. What she didn't know was that this set in motion a line of thinking for me that would define me for most of my life. I made it my life's mission to become a success. This wasn't for personal pride or self-value; it was simply to prove something to the man who didn't want me. I began to envision myself as a James Bond-type of character. I saw myself as a world traveler and an international man of mystery. As a child, I saw myself pulling up to his house in my Trans Am with the T-top open, ringing his doorbell, and asking his name. After he confirmed, I would say, "This is what you missed." I would proceed to throw one hundred bills in the air and peel out of his driveway in my car, kicking rocks in his face. That was it—the driving force was to impress a man who didn't care about me.

Everything I did seemed to be a way to try to impress another man. I tried impress my stepfather to no avail; I never got the love and approval I was seeking. I tried with my football coaches and other male figures in my life until I finally discovered that I was so emotionally deprived that I could never fill the void with human adoration. God had to heal my broken heart and send spiritual fathers into my life to be what I never had. When I turned thirty-nine, I finally learned the truth about my real dad. My mom revealed to me that she had been raped and that I was the product of that horrific act. I felt so sorry for my mother that she had gone through that and that she had carried that for so many years without being able to express it to anyone. For me, it was a tremendous relief; I had been chasing a man who wasn't my real father. It wasn't that he didn't want me; it was that I wasn't his.

I finally discovered that I was so emotionally deprived that I could never fill the void with human adoration. God had to heal my broken heart and send spiritual fathers into my life to be what I never had.

However, gaining this new information didn't mean I had an instant emotional balancing. On the contrary, I had to deal with the fact that the construct I had built my life on was no longer there. What would I do now that I no longer had anyone to impress? What would be my drive and motivating factor? Who would I blame for my failures? What would I do? I did the only thing you can do: I introduced myself to my authentic self. I was tired of the ego-driven path I had followed for so long and made a choice that I would face my darkest fears and explore the depth of who I really was. The results have been life-altering! There is nothing like kicking out the props that have been holding you up, challenging yourself to become a better person, and dealing with those parts of yourself that you would rather ignore.

So what's keeping you awake at night? What recorded messages are playing over and over in your head? You *can* be emotionally balanced. You *can* live a healthy emotional life. Write down what that looks like. Write down what areas you want to change in. Maybe you need more control over anger or fear. Whatever it is, be real and confront yourself. Vision works on an emotional level as well.

There is nothing like kicking out the props that have been holding you up, challenging yourself to become a better person, and dealing with those parts of yourself that you would rather ignore.

Take the time to write out in detail every area of your life that you want to change. Remember, the first step to this type of change is identifying what you really want out of this life, followed by writing it out in detail and dreaming big. Follow this guide on how to lay down the blueprint for your future. You will become whatever you see yourself becoming. Stop here and do it now.

GOALS AND POSITIVE CONFESSIONS

FIVE

GOALS AND
POSITIVE CONFESSIONS

After you have written out your dream, find goals to pursue in your expansive dream. This is where we take the grand dream and break it down into workable parts. Simplicity becomes the next step as we attempt to streamline our wildest dream into something we can wrap our minds around. A dream must begin big, but after that, it needs a foundation to build on. This is one of the main problems when it comes to writing out vision. People have big dreams, but they never go beyond the dream state. The dream seems unattainable because there is nothing to act upon. Mark Twain said, "The secret of getting ahead is getting started."[5] The secret to getting started is breaking down a complex, overwhelming task into small, manageable tasks—and then starting on the first one.

The first step in breaking down the complex and making it simple is finding your targets. These are your goals stated in a simple and concise way. I remember my first experience with goal writing. I was in the military, and I had no concept of vision. My platoon sergeant in California asked me to write out a list of goals and hang it on my wall. I wrote

5. Mark Twain quoted in John C. Maxwell, *Put Your Dream to the Test: 10 Questions to Help You See It and Seize It* (Nashville, TN: Thomas Nelson, 2009), 100.

out the things I wanted to accomplish in the next year. I wrote that I wanted to lose weight, win soldier of the month, make the dean's list at school, and score perfect on my physical fitness test. I can recall waking up every morning, and those goals would "talk" to me. Mind you, I read them only in the morning when I woke and in the evening before I went to sleep. I didn't use any of the techniques in this book. But simply writing down my goals and reading them on a daily basis caused me to experience incredible results. Everything I wrote on that list happened. This step alone can revolutionize your life.

What makes goal writing so powerful? When we understand the way the mind works, we can grasp the principles of goal writing. Writing a goal isn't writing a wish; it's a powerful message sent to the subconscious part of the brain. You see, the first two years of your life are the most impressionable. This is when your outside world that you are completely dependent on is thrust upon you by your caretakers. Your subconscious begins to form patterns about what life really means. This is why many people become exactly like the environment in which they were raised. They are walking out the preset patterns of their subconscious. This download of information continues until the age of seven. During these formative years, a child's mind is said to be in a trancelike state because it operates at a lower frequency of brain activity. This is where reality and imagination merge together.

A prime example of this is something that happened with my daughter recently. One of the twins, Lauren, has a special name for me and her teddy that I bought her a few years ago. She calls me "Dattie" and her bear "Tettie." She has similar affections for both of us. She loves her Dattie and her Tettie. One day, I was playing around with her bear, and I jokingly punched Tettie. When I did this, I punched her a little too hard, sending her flying into the ceiling fan. My daughter grabbed the stuffed animal and began to weep. She's six years old and still operates in that brain capacity to believe that reality and fantasy are one. She really thought I had hurt her stuffed animal.

> If you want different results in your life, you have to engage your mind. Blocks are hindrances not in your spirit but in your mind. You're playing out old patterns that have been set from your childhood.

Interestingly enough, even with my limited knowledge of the vision process, my goals came to pass. You see, I read them every morning when I woke up and every night before I went to bed. Why was this so significant? Brain frequency waves are lowest in the morning and in the evening. So twice a day, your mind mixes reality with fantasy. This is also prime time to download new information into your brain and change old patterns. If you want different results in your life, you have to engage your mind. Blocks are hindrances not in your spirit but in your mind. You're playing out old patterns that have been set from your childhood, and as research now shows, infants in the womb are affected by the emotional states of their mother. I was an unwanted child. This means that I was an unwanted pregnancy. I was rejected from my mother's womb. No wonder I struggled for so many years seeking approval and affirmation. To make lasting changes in your life, you have to engage your mind. The Bible declares in Romans 12:2, *"Be ye transformed by the renewing of your mind."* This change is going to require you to take everything God has placed in your spirit and allow it to be impregnated in your mind. Let's look at how to begin this process.

Finding Goals within Your Vision

Scan the first category that you wrote in your vision. This section covers your spiritual life, your connection to God. Can you see a goal in all the words you used to describe your desired relationship? Can you find some simple words that embody all you wrote out in detail? Maybe you described something like this: *I have a close, loving, personal relationship with Jesus. I spend an hour a day in prayer and study of God's Word. What I experience in His presence has an impact on the way I live my life.* A good goal could look something like this: a close, personal relationship with Jesus. See how simple and concise that is? What you're doing is taking all the information you described and turning it into something you can grasp with your mind. Instead of writing out a goal as long as a paragraph, you have all the information captured in a short statement. You may be like me and feel like everything you wrote down will be forgotten, but don't worry—your goal is backed by a detailed vision, and your mind will consciously and unconsciously work out what you wrote. Sometimes you may even want to go back and read over your vision to reinforce your goal in your mind.

Next, you want to do the same thing for your close relationships with your family. You may have written something like, *My wife and I have a passionate, supportive, and close connection. We're not only completely in love but also best friends.* A good goal for this would be a happy and loving marriage. This is a simple way to state the detailed vision you wrote out earlier, and it captures all you want to say in a short phrase. Here's an example of how you may want to list your goals:

1. Close relationship with Jesus

2. Happy and loving marriage

3. Success at _____ (e.g., preaching)

4. Success at earning _____

5. Buying the perfect home

6. Reaching a healthy weight of _____

The key to writing goals is to summarize the words that best capture your vision.

In the army, I had no written, expansive dream; neither did I have any of the other tools that I'll be sharing with you as we progress through this book. All I had were goals that I wanted to accomplish over the next year and half. I remember very distinctly how all this came about. When I got to California from Germany, where I had been a good soldier and accomplished quite a bit, I knew my time was limited, and I decided to do the bare minimum to get done and get out. This is very uncharacteristic of me. Nonetheless, I went through the first two months, gained weight, could've care less how I scored on my physical fitness test, and didn't care how I was viewed. One day in my room, I heard the Holy Spirit say to me, "What if you don't waste your time but make the most out of it?" I accepted the challenge and decided to make immediate changes.

I started working on my weight first. I dropped from 220 to 175 pounds. I started studying for promotion boards and went back to school. I made a list of things I wanted to accomplish in the time I had left, and I met every goal before I got out of the military—so much so that they were throwing everything they could at me to try to keep me in the military. I was offered a physician's assistance package that would help me to become an officer. I was given a one-year school drop, during which I would be a full-time student and wouldn't have to come to work. I also would have been allowed to go to two different promotion schools in the meantime. They laid it all out before me because I had accomplished so much from writing out my goals. I turned it all down because I knew my calling was full-time ministry, but through this, I learned the power of goal setting. I can only imagine how much further and faster I could have gone if I knew the next tool I'm about to teach you.

Positive Confessions

For many people, positive confessions seem like New Age catchphrases, but I assure you they are so much more than that, and they are as biblical as any other concept in the Bible. The power of speaking is seen right from the beginning, when God spoke the world into existence. In the Genesis narrative and throughout the Bible, we see the power of words. Let's look at some Scriptures before I show you how to put this teaching into practice.

Job 22:28 says, *"Thou shalt also decree a thing, and it shall be established unto thee: and the light shall shine upon thy ways."* In this verse, we see the power of speaking a thing—anything. In fact, I want to suggest to you that you are what you've been speaking over the course of your life. What you speak is what you become. The things you've been experiencing are happening because you have put your thoughts into words. You have been decreeing what you think (whether good or bad). These words are being established in your life. That's why you must first change the way you think so you can change the way you speak. When you change the way you speak, you change what is established in your life.

> What you speak is what you become. The things you've been experiencing are happening because you have put your thoughts into words. You have been decreeing what you think (whether good or bad). These words are being established in your life. That's why you must first change the way you think so you can change the way you speak.

These decrees become the spotlight to the path of your future. If you think about sickness and all that could negatively happen to your health, you will being speaking it. What you say will keep opening up paths for sickness in your life. Proverbs 18:21 puts it this way: *"Death and life are in the power of the tongue: and they that love it shall eat the fruit thereof."* It's interesting that death is listed first in this verse. I believe this is intentional because we all have the natural inclination to speak negativity. That's why we have so much negativity showing up in our lives. This verse says that we will eat the fruit of what comes from of our mouth. What happens when we change our self-talk? What happens when we decide to speak God's Word over our lives? What happens when we speak our dreams into existence? Good begins to show up. When we speak life, that's exactly what we get—life! Who would have ever thought that our words could have so much power over our experience? God did, because He set up the process of manifestation this way. Romans 4:17 (AKJV) says that He *"calls those things which be not as though they were."*

We, too, have the power to look at an impossible situation and speak what we want to happen instead of what we see. You have been empowered to open your mouth and change your circumstances. This is the primary reason why we wrote out our vision and turned that vision into simple goals. The goals are written to express in positive confessions. Hebrews 10:23 says, *"Hold fast the profession of [your] faith without wavering."* *"Profession"* is translated from the Greek word meaning "confession," so the writer is saying that we should hold fast to the confession of our faith. It's so important to understand that faith speaks, and it declares what we believe. Second Corinthians 4:13 says, *"We having the same spirit of faith, according as it is written, I believed, and therefore have I spoken; we also believe, and therefore speak."* When we put this all together, we understand that we are speaking people who have the power to declare what we believe rather than what we see. Most of us have spent our entire life speaking what we see instead of what we would like to see. This is where the power of positive confession comes in. We don't speak death but life; we don't speak lack but abundance; we don't speak sickness but health. You have tremendous power in your words, and I'm going to show you how to unlock its full potential.

Before we take that step, it's important to know how to speak what you want to see. We serve an eternal God. When something is eternal, it has no beginning, no ending, and never loses its power. You see, God is an eternal *now*. He's a God of right now, and faith is always spoken where God is. We speak our goals by faith because their fulfillment is set in the future. Faith is always in the now. Hebrews 11:1 says, *"Now faith is the substance of things hoped for, the evidence of things not seen."* The key to speaking anything by faith is to speak it now. You have to literally speak it as if you already have it, even though this is true only from a spiritual perspective. Another word for confession is *affirmation*, which is a Latin term meaning "to make firm." What you speak by faith now first becomes firm in the spiritual realm. It's only a matter of time until what's firm in the spiritual realm becomes firm in the natural.

We must understand how the mind works and that we need to use words that the mind can work with. We are going to speak as if we presently have what we believe. We want to let our minds know that this is a work in progress, so we are going to use words like *succeeding*. This gives us the now effect but keeps the element of truth present in the confession. Here are some examples of confessions with the goals from earlier in this chapter:

1. I am now succeeding at a close relationship with Jesus.

2. I am now succeeding at a loving, supportive marriage.

3. I am now succeeding at preaching and doing what I love to do.

4. I am now succeeding at earning $200,000 a year.

5. I am now succeeding at buying the perfect home.

6. I am now succeeding at reaching a healthy weight of 180 pounds.

You may have as little as ten confessions or as many as twenty—that doesn't matter, as long as you are writing them based on your goals and speaking them now. Remember that the two best times to speak your goals are when you first wake up and right before you go to sleep. This is when your imagination mixes with reality, causing you to really believe that these things are happening in your life. With that being said, you should speak these confessions as frequently as possible. I have a copy of my confessions in my money clip, and I pull them out as often as time affords to speak them over my life.

People have asked me how I always seem to land on my feet and how I'm able to focus on something and it happens. I always have a written vision, and I speak it as if were already a present reality. I'm not special; these biblical principles can work for you just as they work for me.

When I became dedicated to the vision process, I decided that I was going to walk out this process and let the chips fall where they might regardless of my fears and doubts. I remember having no preaching engagements, but I had a confession. I would speak the following confession every day: "I am now traveling the world preaching the Word." I had no plane ticket, no prospects, and no phone calls, but I believed in the vision I had written out and I spoke in faith. I noticed that the more

I spoke my confessions, the better I felt and the more I had this feeling that it could actually happen. Then I started seeing things lining up, bringing to pass what I spoke.

Confessions activate your spirit and, perhaps more importantly, engage your mind. Your mind can grow and change with active engagement. When you speak positive confessions out of your mouth, you begin to fuse new synapses in your mind that affect your belief system. You can literally change belief systems by simply speaking something new. As we use our cerebral energy to say what we want to happen instead of accept what has always happened, then we can affect positive change in our lives. You will become what you believe—nothing more and nothing less. So what do you do if your belief systems are wrong? You write out a new plan for your life, you find the new goals or targets that you want to shoot for, and then you turn them into confessions that you speak every day, as often as you can.

> You can literally change belief systems by simply speaking something new. As we use our cerebral energy to say what we want to happen instead of accept what has always happened, then we can affect positive change in our lives.

Confessions have a tremendous impact on the way we think, and what we think holds the key to what we believe. If you change your words, you change your thoughts. When you change your thoughts, you change your self-talk. When you tell yourself what you want to be producing instead of what you are producing, you will experience sweeping change in your old, limited belief system. Your current state of life may be directly connected to your belief system. The good news is that through using daily confessions, you can start to change the old, habitual thinking that's been keeping you from living at the highest levels.

What you say to yourself is so important. Your communication with yourself determines how you view yourself in the world. It affects what you can do, be, and have in this world. If you believe that you'll always be sick, then you will. If you believe that you will never be anything more than what your family history says you can be, then that's exactly what will happen. If you believe that you'll always be broke, then you will always be broke.

I came from a very hardworking family. I'm thankful for their labor and the sacrifice of their time so that my basic needs could be met. We didn't always eat what we wanted to eat, but we ate, and I'm thankful for that. We never seemed to have enough money. I can remember going into the store and asking for a certain item, only to hear, "We don't have enough money for that." This was a true statement; we didn't have enough, but I can recall thinking that if my parents worked all the time, then that should produce more than enough. Instead, they worked all the time, and we never had enough. My stepfather would wake up at 3:30 A.M. every morning to go to his job at the steel mill. My mom would work late into the night doing hair, but we still had lack. I began to imagine the possibility of living a different life. I would think to myself, *Certainly there must be a way to do what I love and make more than enough doing it.* There had to be a different way.

As I watched the people around me slowly integrate into the normalcy of their environment, I dreamed of something different. I dreamed of living a truly satisfying life that could provide an abundance of recourses. This type of thinking brought me to the place I am now. Mind you, there was a lot of trial and error, and I failed many times, but I never gave up on my dream. This quest eventually led me to learning how to write out a vision for my life that would forever alter my life. I want to put you on the fast track. I don't want you to continue down the same path of trial and error. There will be adjustments and difficulties along the way, but at least you will have what I didn't have—a clear, written vision, with confessions to accompany what you believe.

At a young age, I thought, *I don't have to be like everyone else; I can do something, and I can be something different than my environment. I don't have to live here for the rest of my life; I can change my scenery and my circle of influence.* This shift in consciousness started me down the path to finding that different thing I was searching for. The only thing I was lacking was a more direct and deliberate path to what I desired. Once I discovered the vision process, I not only could pinpoint what I desired but could also speak what I desired. Using the power of positive confession, I saw miraculous changes in my life. I went from being a local preacher to traveling the world speaking on some of the largest platforms—all because I spoke what I wanted to happen in my life. I spoke what I knew God had destined for me to be. You, too, have this power in your mouth. You can speak into existence what you see in your spirit and believe in your mind. The power of confession is limitless!

> You can speak into existence what you see in your spirit and believe in your mind. The power of confession is limitless!

It's important to understand that confessions aren't limited to what you've written down in your vision. In fact, the best use of positive confessions is the Word of God. The Bible is so full of powerful truths that you can adopt them, speak them, and literally shape your future. Scripture says, *"Whereby are given to us exceeding great and precious promises: that by these you might be partakers of the divine nature"* (2 Peter 1:4 AKJV). It's so important to understand that the Bible is filled with promises for every part of your life. It is your right according to the Word to become a partaker of these exceedingly great promises. You can easily apply Scriptures as confessions in your everyday life. The way you become more like God is to speak what He says you are. After you discover what God says about you in His Word, you must speak it. The Word of God is two mouths, God's mouth and your mouth. Let's take a moment and find out how to use the Word of God as the basis of our confessions.

The Word of God is so amazing because it covers every area of your life and can be used as a tool to produce different results in your life than what you are currently experiencing. Let's look at some common problems and what the Word says about them, and how we can bring lasting change in our lives.

I'm going to start with a subject that all of us have experienced at some point in our lives and that some of you may be dealing with as you read this book. That topic is a lack of peace. Perhaps one of the most difficult things to deal with is when you can't find a place of rest and tranquility. There's nothing quite like staying awake all night, worried about something, and then repeating the cycle the next night all because you can't find that place of peace. Let's look at some Scriptures that deal with peace and how we can apply them to our lives so we can experience God's indescribable peace.

I'll start with the Scripture that helped me in one of the lowest seasons of my life. I remember the day—I was lying flat on the floor on my face. I was living in Oakland, California, and my life was in shambles. I had no direction, no vision, and no plan. I didn't know what to do with my life, and I felt all alone. As I lay on the floor, I remember the sinking feeling in the pit of my stomach—a feeling as if my life was over before it had started. I could see myself struggling with depression about my future. The trepidation about the lack of peace felt completely overwhelming. As I was trying to make some type of connection with my Creator, I heard a voice speaking to my spirit. God spoke His Word to me, but it was incomplete. He reminded me of Isaiah 26:3: *"Thou wilt keep him in perfect peace, whose mind is stayed on thee."* Then I heard Him say, "That's not all; take out your Bible and read the whole verse." I looked up the passage and saw what I had been missing: *"Because he trusteth in thee."*

I found one of the greatest keys to peace. Peace comes when you trust God with your past, present, and future. You have to trust that He had a plan for everything you have gone through. You have to trust that He knows exactly where you are now and that He is working every area of your life to bring about a better future. Right then, I heard Him speak a third time. He said, "Your problem is that you don't trust Me anymore." I realized in that moment that I was trying to work out my life. I understood that my methods weren't working simply because I was trying to do it on my own, independent from God. I had been wounded, hurt, and crushed from my childhood. I didn't realize that I was blaming God for my troubles and taking out the one factor that had the power to bring me out. I didn't know it at the time, but I was going on my own while still going through the motions of religious activity. I was going to church and punching the ticket, but I had no real relationship with God. The reason was simple—inwardly I blamed Him for where I was in my life. When I read Isaiah 26:3 in its entirety, I understood exactly what the problem was. I was going through the motions but still doing things without God because I thought He was the source of my problems.

Maybe you can identify with this. You may know what it's like to look like you have it all together. You go to church, you're involved in religious activities, but you're dying inside. If so, then it's time to get your peace back. I want you to make this positive confession of the Word of God in your life:

Father, in the name of Jesus, I confess Isaiah 26:3 over my life. I am now in perfect peace, my mind is stayed on You, and I completely trust You.

I learned another great Scripture that deals with peace in Sunday school as a member of the Church of God in Christ. We would always begin each class by reciting a few Scriptures. I prided myself for being so faithful to Sunday school and for not needing to read the Scriptures to recite them. Although I had them memorized, they hadn't become a source of strength, and I certainly didn't use them as a means for daily positive confessions. It wasn't until later in life that I took one of those memorized Scriptures and made it a part of my repertoire of verses on peace. That verse that I so faithfully spoke every Sunday morning until it was etched into my mind was Colossians 3:15, which reads, *"Let the peace of God rule in your hearts, to the which also ye are called in one body;*

and be ye thankful." Before we turn this verse into a positive confession, let's look at the power contained in the words. The first part of this verse reads, *"Let the peace of God rule in your hearts."* The *Amplified Bible* says that peace is like an umpire, ruling out good and evil. So the peace that God gives us should act as a discerning voice that indicates what we should or shouldn't do in any given moment.

Have you ever heard someone say, "I don't have a peace about that"? This is the power of peace. If you don't have it in any given area, then it's a good indication that you shouldn't make a move in that area of your life. Peace acts as an umpire, ruling in our hearts and helping us make the right choices as we pray. Peace is the deciding factor on whether we should take action. If you don't have peace, don't do it! The verse goes on to say, *"Be ye thankful."* This is so vitally important as it relates to having peace in your life. Thankfulness is a major factor.

This leads me to the next verse on peace and how thankfulness plays a part in the concept of peace. Scripture says,

> *In nothing be anxious; but in everything by prayer and supplication with thanksgiving let your request be made known unto God. And the peace of God, which passeth all understanding, shall guard your hearts and your thoughts in Christ Jesus.* (Philippians 4:6–7 ASV)

In this verse, we see that anxiety takes the center stage as one of the enemies of our peace. The King James Version uses *"careful"* instead of *"anxious."* This is translated from the Greek word *merimnaō*, which means to be anxious, troubled with cares, and to take thought. This word helps us understand what anxiety does to us and how it affects our level of peace. When we are unsure about something, we can slip into doubt. This doubt grows into a fear, and fear creates an anxious mind-set about our present or future circumstances. Anxiety can be completely crippling as it relates to our spiritual and mental stability.

If you desire to live a life of peace, you must first confront what you're afraid of. This begins with a process. You must first identify what the source of your fear is, then you must work to eradicate that fear.

You may need to seek some counseling to have a sounding board and to develop a plan for anxiety. The steps you can take begin with identifying the problem, as previously stated. Where has this fear come from? Has a traumatic event affected your faith and belief that God could help you in whatever you face? Has someone let you down in a relationship? Have you suffered a financial setback? Do you wonder how God could have let you go through that? I have found that anxiety always has a root cause, and it's usually something that has placed you in a position of doubt in God's ability to help you. If this is you, simply follow the instructions in Philippians 4:6: *"In nothing be anxious."* But how? *"By prayer and supplication with thanksgiving."*

The writer of this verse first engages us on the general idea of prayer. Start with seeking God and finding a connection with Him in prayer. Something that works for me might work for you—I literally write out my prayers. I use Philippians 4:6–7 as a general guide. The first thing I do is start with prayer. What type of prayer do I start with? I start with worship. I do as David did—I write poems unto God through worship. I spend time in complete adoration of and adulation for God. I try to take myself out of the scenario and make it all about Him. My prayer begins like this:

> Father, You are so wonderful. You are incredible, You are an awesome God, and You are excellent. You are worthy of all the glory, honor, and praise. Your name is great and greatly to be praised. You are the King of Kings and the Lord of Lords. You are the Lily of the Valley, the Bright and Morning Star.

You can see that I begin in prayer with adoration. It flows so easily because it's a daily practice of mine. You see, it's so important that you get in contact with God right from the beginning. There is no better way to come into His presence than to worship and honor Him. From this place of worship, I enter into confession. This is when I admit and confess all I have done wrong. I also ask for forgiveness through repentance.

Next, I go into thanksgiving. I can't tell you how important this is, not only as a cure for anxiety, but also as a way to create hope for the future. So many times, we are so wrapped up in the cares of this life that we find it hard to stop and be thankful for what we have. I admit that this seems a little counterintuitive; why would we be thankful when we're not producing the results we desire? You see, being thankful is a method for multiplication. Being thankful for what you have can bring more of what you want into your life. We see this in the story of the fish and the loaves of bread. Scripture says, *"Jesus took the loaves; and when he had given thanks, he distributed to the disciples, and the disciples to them that were set down; and likewise of the fishes as much as they would"* (John 6:11). You see, celebration always brings multiplication. This word *"thanks"* is translated from the Greek word *eucharisteo*, which means to be grateful and to express gratitude. Jesus took two fish and five loaves of bread and fed over five thousand people—and He had twelve baskets of leftovers, all because He gave thanks.

So many times, we look at what we have and focus on how small it is in comparison to what we desire in our life. The first key to changing a life of lack is to learn to give thanks; thanksgiving will multiply what you're thankful for. This can even be employed on a prophetic basis. You can be thankful for what you don't have as if you already had it. You can thank God in advance for the home you desire, the job you've dreamed about, or the right type of relationship. All of this can happen through the power of thanksgiving.

> We look at what we have and focus on how small it is in comparison to what we desire in our life. The first key to changing a life of lack is to learn to give thanks; thanksgiving will multiply what you're thankful for. This can even be employed on a prophetic basis.

Paul said that the peace of God is found not only in prayer and thanksgiving but also in supplication. Supplication isn't independent of prayer but rather another a form of prayer. Supplication is translated from the Greek word *deesis*, which means to make petition. We should make our requests known unto God. This is so important to our peace because this is the time when we stop carrying all the pressure of our unpaid bills. We stop worrying about our health challenges. We finally rest at night from thoughts about our relationships never working. This is when we ask God for the needs of our lives to be met. This is when we put our desires before God.

When you feel overwhelmed, you have a place you can go. You can make your request known to a living God who wants to help you out in every area of your life. If you follow this pattern, God will give you the peace that passes all understanding. (See Philippians 4:7.) This has a twofold meaning. The first is that God has a peace that is beyond your comprehension. God's peace goes beyond any emotion you could ever have, any felling you could ever experience. It's knowing that everything is going to work out just fine. It's an amazing feeling to know that you already have secured victory in your life before you actually see the manifestation. The other meaning of this word is peace that transcends your ability to understand your situation. Things can come at you from all different directions at times, and it may be difficult to understand why all this is happening to you. God gives you a peace that goes beyond your ability to understand why you are in what you're in. You may not be able to wrap your mind around your current problem, but God has a peace that can cause you to believe that it will work for your good, even when all signs are pointing in the opposite direction.

In fact, the word *"peace"* in this verse is translated from the Greek word *eirene*, which means prosperity, one, quietness, rest, and to set at one again. To experience this peace that passes all understanding is to pray about your pain, your struggles, your finances, your marriage, and everything in your life. When you do, you will feel that prosperity is coming to you. You'll be at one with yourself and God again, and you will quietly rest from all the burdens you've shouldered for so long. The amazing thing about it all is that this is available to you every day of your life. Using Philippians 4:6–7 and Colossians 3:15 as confessions may look something like this:

Father, in the name of Jesus, I decree and declare that I am now being ruled by the peace of God in my heart, and I am thankful. I decree and declare that I am now succeeding at being free from anxiety. I pray to You and make my request known, and You give me the peace that passes all understanding.

Just as you can make positive confessions with your goals, you can make positive confessions with the Word of God to cover every area of your life. Let's take a look at how you can use God's Word to make confessions about healing for your body. Third John 2 says, *"Beloved, I wish above all things that thou mayest prosper and be in health, even as thy soul prospereth."* This is one of my favorite confession Scriptures simply because it covers more than just healing. This is a verse of balance in the way it deals with your prosperity, your health, and your soul, which is a reference to your mind in this verse.

God is certainly concerned with everything that concerns you. In fact, Psalm 138:8 says, *"The LORD will perfect that which concerneth me."* Again, the Word says, *"No good thing will he withhold from them that walk uprightly"* (Psalm 84:11 ASV). Before we deal with this verse in its totality and reveal proper confessions for this verse, let's take a look at what this verse tells us about healing. This verse is unique in that it doesn't deal with healing but with health. This passage unlocks God's true desire for our lives regarding a healthy lifestyle. God's original design wasn't for us to be on a rollercoaster of health. So many times, we are sick, then healed; sick, then healed. It seems like a never-ending cycle. It's important to know that we all will face challenges, and many of us will face them in the area of our health—but we have some tools available to us to change the course of how well we live.

God wants us to break the cycle of sickness in our lives and bring divine health.

In 3 John 2, John doesn't wish that we would be healed; he wishes that we may *"be in heath."* God wants us to break the cycle of sickness in our lives and bring divine health. What if we could live a long, healthy life? Would we take that? According to 3 John 2, if we properly apply this verse, that's exactly what we can have. Make this an everyday part of your confessions—that you will live in God's divine health. I have a habit of speaking healing over myself when I feel perfectly fine. Why? Because I want to let sickness know that I'm healed before it ever shows up. You may ask if I ever get sick, and the answer is yes. However, I have more healthy days than sick days. Just like with anything else, I attribute this to my daily confessions. The key is to be proactive and not reactive, to be on the offense and not the defense. I would rather speak health over myself even when I feel good than wait until I'm sick to start speaking.

Let's take a moment to bring balance to this concept. It's also important to take into account your responsibility. You cannot eat bad food and never exercise and still think that you are going to be healthy. If your diet consists of fried foods and sweets, then you are destined to have health challenges regardless of what you speak. Scripture tells us, *"Faith, if it has not works, is dead"* (James 2:17 AKJV). This simply means that you have to put action to your faith. This means having a daily routine of healthy eating and exercise. God will heal your body, but it's up to you to do your part in making sure you take care of the natural part of the supernatural. I make confessions over my health every day. I also watch what I eat, and I'm an avid runner. As you speak faith over your health, also be proactive about maintaining a healthy lifestyle.

John's main concern in 3 John 2 is that we prosper. This has a lot to do with our health as well. When our finances are down, or when we are drowning in debt, it affects not only our standard of living but also our health. Stress is one of the most dangerous things a person can deal with, and nothing brings more stress than worrying about money. So John is telling us that he wants to see us prosper. I know we have talked at some length about money, but I think it's so important to understand that God doesn't enjoy seeing us struggle. On the contrary, "[He] *has pleasure in the prosperity of his servant"* (Psalm 35:27 AKJV).

John's last point in 3 John 2 involves his statement concerning the mind. The words *"even as thy soul prospereth"* carry a lot of weight. It's important that we all accept and understand that our minds play a major role in our spiritual walk. I work with a group of addicts, and one of the main areas of focus is understanding that their addiction started out as a poor spiritual decision but has turned into a mental condition. People want to stop a number of bad habits. They even pray about it, with no change. They are caught up in false repentance, when they repent because they feel bad but they know they're going to do it again. Why? Because they haven't experienced change of mind. All true theology requires psychology. That's why the Bible says, *"Be renewed in the spirit of your mind"* (Ephesians 4:23). Romans 12:2 says, *"Be ye transformed by the renewing of your mind."* Breaking habits and changing beliefs must be done on a mental level. The problem this poses for most people is that they have to face their problem and limited beliefs. They have to be willing to gain the proper information and make changes on a mental level. Much of this work is done through the repetitious work of confession. They have to visualize what they desire to be and speak it out of their mouth every day. The most effective and transformative way to do this is by speaking the Word of God over their life. What we say becomes inculcated in our minds, and, sooner or later, we will see the words changing the way we think. When we change our thoughts, our actions soon follow. Let's look at what 3 John 2 looks like as a confession:

> Father, in the name of Jesus, I decree and declare that, according to 3 John 2, above all things, I prosper, I am in health, and my mind prospers.

Isaiah 53:5 says, *"But he was wounded for our transgressions, he was bruised for our iniquities: the chastisement of our peace was upon him; and with his stripes we are healed."* This verse not only deals with healing, but it also covers forgiveness. The best way for me to understand a Scripture is to put it into context, break down the words in the original language (which is Hebrew, in this case), and find the purest form of the verse. Let's break down this verse. It begins by telling us that

Jesus was *"was wounded for our transgressions."* *"Wounded"* is translated from the Hebrew word *chalal*, which means "to profane, dishonor, or make common." We often read the word *transgression* in the Bible, but it has little relevance in our modern vernacular. It's translated from the Hebrew word *pasha*, which means revolt or rebellion. So the beginning of Isaiah 53:5 is telling us that Jesus was dishonored and profaned in order to cover our rebellion. Sometimes it's difficult for us to recognize rebellion in our lives. Not only does this cover the original rebellion of Adam, but it also covers our rebellion as believers.

Think about a time when God asked you to do something difficult or face a part of yourself you would rather ignore. Have you ever turned from His instructions? This is rebellion. Thankfully, we can receive forgiveness and restoration by the wounds of Jesus. In fact, many times we rebel because we are wounded. We are hurting and we try to do things independent of God because we don't trust Him. God is so loving that He understands our wounds. He understands what it's like to be hurt, dishonored, and violated. Whatever the source of your wound, whether from your parents or a past relationship, He was wounded for you. His wounds can and will restore you in all the places you feel hurt and violated.

> God is so loving that He understands our wounds. He understands what it's like to be hurt, dishonored, and violated. Whatever the source of your wound, whether from your parents or a past relationship, He was wounded for you. His wounds can and will restore you in all the places you feel hurt and violated.

The next part of this verse says, *"He was bruised for our iniquities"* (Isaiah 53:5). *"Bruised"* is translated from the word *daka*, which means to be crushed, shattered, and broken. *"Iniquities"* is translated from the word *avon*, which means perversity, depravity, or guilt. Jesus was broken and crushed so that we could be healed from perversion, depravity, and guilt. Over the past twenty-one years in ministry, I've noticed that perverse activity is one of the most guilt-ridden activities a person can engage in. Sexual sin is such a stronghold that it puts a person in a personal prison. It has been said that lust is like athlete's foot—the more you scratch it, the more it itches. Not only can God break the bonds of sexual immorality, but He can also relieve your guilt because He has been crushed and broken.

It would be remiss of me not to take a moment and juxtapose the concepts of guilt and shame. They are both from the same family and are covered under Jesus' sacrifice. The difference is found in what they apply to. Feeling guilty is when you feel bad about something you have done. Feeling shame is when you feel bad about who you are as a person. The brokenness Jesus endured is also a healing balm for the wounds of our souls. Perhaps you've been mistreated and abused all your life, so you have a very low value of yourself are as a person. You don't see yourself the way God sees you because of what you've been through. It's time to find out who you are through the Word and speak that Word until it shapes a new self-image. A friend of mine shared some pearls of wisdom with me recently, and I want to express one that really helped me: Forgiveness is giving up hopes for a better past. We often keep alive our pain from the past and relive it as if it were still happening today. In reality, the incident will never change; only our perception of it can change.

If we want to truly heal from the shame and guilt of the past, we have to realize that we can never change the past. We can change only our perception about what the past means to us today. That's why Jesus was broken and crushed, so we could experience freedom from the weight of guilt and shame.

We have to realize that we can never change the past. We can change only our perception about what the past means to us today.

Isaiah goes on to say, *"The chastisement of our peace was upon him"* (Isaiah 53:5). I have talked at length about peace, but I haven't talked about the price that was paid for that peace. Sometimes we take things for granted when we don't fully understand the sacrifice. I have seen this in my own children. I am an incredibly thankful person because I come from so little. I understand lack and struggle, so I'm extremely grateful for God's blessing in my life. My kids, on the other hand, have had a different experience growing up, so my wife and I have to teach them how to be thankful.

It reminds me of the first car I ever had. It was a beat-up, barely running Toyota Celica. I used to have to park that car on a hill, push it down the hill, and pop the clutch to get it started. It was given to me by a neighbor. The funny thing is that I never took care of the car, and it eventually blew up because I never changed the oil. Why would I treat the car that way? Because I didn't have to work for it. When I bought my first car, I washed it several times a week. I did all the regular maintenance because I paid the price for it.

We can know and understand the peace of God but not grasp the level of grief it costed Him. When we do, we will be more thankful and appreciative for our peace. *"Chastisement"* in Isaiah 53:5 is translated from the Hebrew word *muwcar*, which means to be disciplined and corrected. So here we have a sinless being, Jesus Christ, who is subjected to discipline. What an amazing thing that a completely innocent Man would have to endure correction for something He never did. This was all done so that we could have what we spoke of earlier in this chapter: *"peace...which passeth all understanding."*

Finally, Isaiah 53:5 tells us Jesus took lashes across His back for our healing. He took those stripes to alleviate pain in our lives. He took them so we could experience healing from sickness and disease. Use this confession the next time you feel sick or receive a negative doctor's report:

> Father, in Jesus's name, I decree and declare that I am healed right now by the stripes of Jesus according to Isaiah 53:5.

Isaiah 53:5 is a prophetic word from the "eagle eye" prophet. Isaiah was speaking about a future event. He was talking about what would take place on the cross. He says that *"with his stripes we are healed."* This verse takes center stage in another place, in the New Testament after the death, burial, and resurrection of Jesus. First Peter 2:24 says, *"Who his own self bare our sins in his own body on the tree, that we, being dead to sins, should live unto righteousness: by whose stripes ye were healed."* Notice here that Peter speaks about a past event. So when we have a bad test result, a sickness, or an injury, we can believe that we have already been healed. Speaking as if we were already feeling better when we are in the deepest despair of physical pain is a lot to ask, but what other choice do we have?

What you say has a profound effect on your body on a molecular level. Even science has proved that positive words are the breeding ground for healing of all kinds of sickness and injury. If you talk about how bad you feel, it will only amplify and prolong the suffering. When you speak the Word of God over your life, you infuse the power of God's Word to change your situation and open a pathway for the already done—the we *"were healed"* of 1 Peter 2:24. This is why we can speak our healing as a completed work. By His stripes, I'm already healed because "by his stipes we were healed." The stripes Jesus took across His back before His crucifixion were sealed after His death and subsequent resurrection.

Let's look at confessions for our needs and desires. We can use the Scriptures to meet our needs and have our desires manifested in our lives. I often encourage people to work first on their needs and then focus on their desires. This is simply because it's very difficult to dream grand dreams when they can't keep the lights on in their house. Believing to have your needs met is a powerful confidence booster and will produce greater results in your future as you believe for more and speak more over your life.

We all have needs, and needs are ever evolving. There was a time when a car was a desire and not a need. In today's society, most of us can't get to work without a car, so it has become a need. We all need food, clothing, and shelter. Thankfully, God has a plan to take care of our needs. First, He tells us not to worry.

Therefore I tell you, do not worry about your life, what you will eat or drink; or about your body, what you will wear. Is not life more than food, and the body more than clothes? Look at the birds of the air; they do not sow or reap or store away in barns, and yet your heavenly Father feeds them. Are you not much more valuable than they? Can anyone of you by worrying add a single hour to your life? And why do you worry about clothes? See how the flowers of the field grow. They do not labor or spin. Yet I tell you that not even Solomon in all his splendor was dressed like one of these. If that is how God clothes the grass of the field, which is here today and tomorrow is thrown into the fire, will he not much more clothe you—you of little faith? So do not worry, saying, "What shall we eat?" or "What shall we drink?" or "What shall we wear?" For the pagans run after all these things, and your heavenly Father knows that you need them. But seek first his kingdom and his righteousness, and all these things will be given to you as well. Therefore, do not worry about tomorrow, for tomorrow will worry about itself. Each day has enough trouble of its own. (Matthew 6:25–34 NIV)

The overarching theme here is that worrying about your needs is not the path to take. God is telling us that if we simply seek Him and His kingdom principles, all our needs will be taken care of. A great confession of this verse would look like this:

Father, in Jesus's name, I decree and declare that, according to Your Word, I no longer have to worry about my needs. I seek You first, and all my needs are added unto me.

Another good verse about needs is Philippians 4:19, which says, *"My God shall supply all your need according to his riches in glory by Christ Jesus."* I want you to put this book down right now and make a list of all your needs. Then I want you to put them all into a confession using this verse. Your need may be not having enough to make your monthly house payment. You could use this verse as a confession, which may look something like this:

> Father, You promised me in Philippians 4:19 that you would supply all my need. I ask You to supply more than enough to make my monthly mortgage payment in the name of Jesus.

Of course, you can plug any and all your needs into that confession. As you use this confession, watch the tide begin to turn from you. You will go from barely making it to trusting God to meet your every need and watching Him do just that.

Psalm 37:4 says, "*Delight thyself also in the* Lord: *and he shall give thee the desires of thine heart.*" So we see that God certainly wants to go beyond just meeting our needs.

Some Scriptures deal with debt relief. If you have high-interest credit card debt, medical bills, or student loans, these verses can break the hold of debt in your life. Some people don't even realize that God wants them to be debt-free. Scripture speaks of the only debt we should have in life, saying, "*Let no debt remain outstanding, except the continuing debt to love one another, for whoever loves others has fulfilled the law*" (Romans 13:8 niv). Here we clearly see a New Testament verse telling us that we should never have outstanding debts; the only debt we are required to have is the debt of love toward our fellow man. Now I know this may sound elementary, but what do you do when you have debts and don't have enough money to pay them off? Most people would love to be able to live a good lifestyle and be able to pay off all their debts. The problem comes when we have a down season and aren't able to pay our bills. Then we get back to a normal standard of living but don't have enough to pay back what we owe. That's where this confession comes into play. You can speak this as if you already have it and watch the Word take hold and manifest debt freedom in your life. This is what a confession for this verse may look like:

Father, in the name of Jesus, I decree and declare that I have no outstanding debts and that I only have the debt of love toward other people.

Another verse that deals with debt is Deuteronomy 28:12, which says, *"The LORD shall open unto thee his good treasure, the heaven to give the rain unto thy land in his season, and to bless all the work of thy hand: and thou shalt lend unto many nations, and thou shalt not borrow."* This verse may seem outdated unless you are a farmer and your crops and income are dependent on the weather in your life. So how does this agricultural Scripture fit into the mold of modern life? Most of us don't own farms or make our living based on the seasons of reaping and sowing. However, this verse isn't obsolete for us today. In fact, it is just as relevant today as it was when it was written. Just because our type of work has shifted from agricultural to industrial to digital doesn't negate the impact of this Scripture. We have the same need for shelter, food, and clothing as any other generation before us. This passage can easily be plugged into our lives and be used regardless of our occupation. We see in Deuteronomy 28:12 that God has a *"good treasure."* The word *"good"* in this verse means "rich, valuable in estimation." *"Treasure"* means "storehouse, store, supplies of food or drink, treasury, gold or silver." So we see that God wants to open up His riches that are stored up for us.

This flies in the face of the belief that God wants us to barely make it or to only have our needs met. God is a God of abundant overflow, and He has a treasure on reserve for us all to enjoy. I've heard people say that they don't care about money, which reminds me of a line from the film Aviator, in which Leonardo DiCaprio, playing the part of Howard Hughes, is sitting at the table with his love interest and her family. The mother says to him, "We don't care about money," to which he replies, "That's because you've always had it." Don't get me wrong, I don't think you should organize your life around money, but you should have more than enough to take care of yourself and your family, enjoy your life, and also be able to give back. This Scripture explicitly tells us that there is more than enough in God's supply.

The text continues by saying that rain will come at the proper season. You have to understand that life is a seasonal journey. We will deal with ups and downs and changes along the way. Circumstances will change, but our resolve must remain the same. When we live a principle-centered life that's connected to the Word of God, we will have amazing outcomes. Speak the Word over your life in good seasons and in bad seasons because all seasons change. When they change, you want them to manifest what you believe in your vision and in the Word of God so you can find good success. You have to know that when everything around you seems dry, God's rain will eventually return. When it returns, you want to be found saying what God is saying, not speaking what you see happing during a low time. Many times, we extend a season based off what we say. We're not sure about our confession of faith because it looks as if it's not working, so we allow ourselves to confirm what our life is currently showing instead of what God has promised us in our future. It's in these times that we have to refocus. We have to turn back to our faith and speak what we believe, not what we see or feel. We have to know that God, like the weather, never allows a season to remain forever. We must know this when we are in a good season as well. Part of the reason for a good season is to get us what we need to make it through the other seasons of life. It's important that we properly manage seasons so we are always functioning well.

> Speak the Word over your life in good seasons and in bad seasons because all seasons change. When they change, you want them to manifest what you believe in your vision and in the Word of God so you can find good success. You have to know that when everything around you seems dry, God's rain will eventually return.

Last, this verse tells us that we will *"lend unto many nations, and thou shalt not borrow"* (Deuteronomy 28:12). This is an amazing promise! In a society that is weighed down with student loans, house payments, car loans, and credit card debt, this seems impossible. We can look at this from a national perspective as a promise to Israel that they would be a lending, not a borrowing, nation. The United States was and is in many ways this type of nation. We are dealing with a national debt that is out of control, but it wasn't always that way. This is not the plan God has for any nation that stands on His Word, and it's not His idea for His people either. To make this less global and more personal, let's take a different approach.

The Hebrew word for *"nations"* in this verse is *gowy*, which means "a nation not of Hebrew origin." This simply means that Israel was to lend to people who were not in their family and that they were not to borrow. We, too, should become lenders and not borrowers. Of course, the most efficient way to do this is to be out of debt and to have enough surplus that you can lend to others. On the surface, this verse seems to be self-explanatory, but it has a deeper spiritual truth that transcends money. The Hebrew word for *"lend"* in Deuteronomy 28:12 is *lavah*, which means to twine, unite, join, or to be joined. So this promise extends beyond just lending money to other nations; it carries the connotation of invitation. How so? There is an invitation here for other nations to join the family, for us to lend or give our experience with God to the world and to bring in people who need healing, forgiveness, and redemption. We are to be connected to people who are in need and may not look like us or have the same customs as we do. We are to invite them in to join in this most powerful covenant of grace and blessing. Here's a way to use this verse as a positive confession of the Word of God:

> I am now succeeding at being completely debt-free. I am a lender and not a borrower in Jesus's name.

If you are like me, then your desires extend beyond debt relief. Once you have spoken these verses over your life to fulfill your needs and to bring you out of debt, speak biblical desires for your life. Proverbs 13:22 (AKJV) says, *"A good man leaves an inheritance to his children's children: and the wealth of the sinner is laid up for the just."* This verse is so powerful because it literally extends beyond you. I'm not only interested in prosperity for myself, but I want a sense of knowing that the generations to follow won't have to start out like me. I have no inheritance, no wealth transfer to call my own, but I have endeavored to break that cycle and change the next generations in my family. I believe that God's will is to leave prosperity and a legacy to our children that extends even to their kids. I know that many of you reading this book are wondering how you're going to make it to the next paycheck and can't wrap your mind around anything beyond what's in front of you. But what if you could take a moment and picture yourself in a different place, one that's filled with abundance that will outlive you?

That's the whole purpose of this book and of this chapter on confessions, to get you to see something greater than where you are and to chart a course for how to get there. You don't have to live in a constant struggle. There are promises just like this that share with you the core belief that you can have a better, more abundant, and totally satisfying life. The reason these verses are so important is because they have the power to change your old patterns of belief and mold new ones. The power of language as it relates to human beings has been studied for years—it's the one thing that separates us from the animal kingdom. We can reason, be self-aware, and speak about our experiences. But so many times we are self-saboteurs of our own future by speaking about our problems instead of God's solutions for our life. It's time to say good-bye to the days of wallowing in your misery and pain and rise up and do something about it.

So many times we are self-saboteurs of our own future by speaking about our problems instead of God's solutions for our life. It's time to say good-bye to the days of wallowing in your misery and pain and rise up and do something about it.

I don't want you to speak these confessions as if you were just going through the motions. I want you to visualize yourself meeting your goals and feel what it's going to be like when that dream comes to pass or that Scripture verse manifests in your present reality. Let God's Word sink down into every fiber of your being. Use your God-given power of language to speak yourself out of bad situations and speak yourself into good ones. Use the verse shared above as a confession:

> I am now succeeding at having more than enough so that my kids and grandkids can live off my wealth.

There are so many verses I could share about peace, freedom, love, happiness, wealth, and many other topics. There is no shortage of material in Scripture to address every concern and care. I have started you on the path, and I suggest that you use a concordance or simply Google search for Scriptures and formulate confessions using the pattern shared in this chapter.

There is one more vital principle as it relates to the power of positive confessions. Some churches teach that emotion hinders rather than helps us. It is certainly true that we shouldn't allow our emotions to control us, but that doesn't mean we shouldn't feel or understand them. Emotions have been demonized and sacrificed on the altar of spirituality. For some reason, the belief has crept in that if we give place to emotions, we are not spiritual. I believe that this is a mishandling of emotions; they should be noticed and used in the art of confession.

Today, we still use emotions for spiritual explanations. How many times have you heard someone say, "I feel like things are going to work out"? Perhaps you have heard someone say that, after an exhilarating worship experience, they felt the Spirit. Spiritualism and emotions go hand in hand. How does this apply to confessions? You can use your powerful ability to be self-aware and think to yourself what it would feel like to have desire. Perhaps you can think about a time when you felt peace; use that memory to fuel your future feelings. Perhaps you have no past point of reference, but you can think about how it might feel if everything worked out. When you tie strong emotion to your confessions, you send a powerful message to your mind that you will one day feel what you are saying. The more you can bring future feeling into your present confession, the stronger the impact. It's important to visualize what you are believing and confessing and see yourself as if you already had it. Ask yourself how this would look and feel to you. Become excited about it as if you already had it. This may seem new to you, but this is actually an older concept in church. Most of us have heard someone say to give God praise for something as if it has already happened. Why? Because this is a powerful exercise of faith. It says to your emotions that you are already in possession of this thing right now and that it is as good as yours.

> It's important to visualize what you are believing and confessing and see yourself as if you already had it. Ask yourself how this would look and feel to you. Become excited about it as if you already had it. This may seem new to you, but this is actually an older concept in church.

To review, we have learned that we can take the goals we pulled from our overall vision and turn them into positive confessions that we speak on a daily basis. As we do this, we begin to formulate ideas and plans on how to accomplish these goals, which we will talk about in the next chapter. For now, focus on speaking what's in your head and written down on paper. Along with confessing your dream, you can also go directly to the Word of God and speak what He says about us in Scripture. Be sure to always speak them in the now as if you already have them, and remember Romans 4:17 (AKJV), which says that we have the power to "[call] *those things which be not as though they were.*"

It can seem a bit strange to speak what we desire to happen and not what is happening. This is understandable because we have been conditioned to look at the negative side of things. Unless you came from a home that understood and practiced these principles, then you are bound to focus on what is instead of what can be. Daily positive confessions about your goals and using the Word of God as the center of your speaking can revolutionize what happens in your future. I've spent a great deal of time on this subject because I know what it can produce and the profound impact it can have on all those who practice it. You can change the way you see your world and the hope you have for a better future by using the power of words.

A PLAN

SIX

A PLAN

Everything in this world is governed by a design, which follows a certain pattern or plan. Every child comes into this world after nine months of development. Crops are harvested after placing seed in the ground and caring for the plants. There is a master design behind every living organism on the planet. I am fully informed of the idea of natural selection and the thought that we evolved into what we are. I find it hard to take intelligence out of the equation and to leave it all up to chance. Things are not that random; instead, I see the careful structure and plan of a master Creator. I see a specific design and purpose in every living thing. I think it is particularly important to understand that humans were created for an even higher purpose. Each of us has a genetic code that predisposes us to certain things, and God's download of our calling begins in this code. It is up to us to seek God for that high calling and plan for the fulfillment of it. None of us are here just to exist; we all were put here for a reason, and this book is a tool to help you unlock what that is.

One of the most important things you can do is have a plan. When you write a plan for your vision, you are following in the footsteps of the master Planner. To plan is to take the highest dream you can have and support it with smaller goals that will lead you to the ultimate goal. The key to moving from a positive confession to manifestation is having a plan. Plans move you from what you think and say to what you do.

In the end, your beliefs are made real only when followed by action. You have to do something! You can't speak into the atmosphere and expect change if you don't take action. In fact, the faster you take action, the sooner you will see change. Many times, we say we are waiting on God for a change when He is waiting on us to make a move. Movement is the key to realizing all that you can conceive in your mind. Many say that they can't imagine certain things. Don't be that person! You can imagine a better life for you and your family. You can imagine a better living situation, business, or career. You can imagine it; the next question is, what will you do about it?

When you wrote out your dream, that's exactly what you were doing. You were imagining something better. Your goals became the targets you wanted to hit, and then you turned those goals into something you say on a daily basis—confessions. Now it's time to do what it takes to see your dreams come true. A plan will set in motion what you need to do to reach your highest calling in life. So let's find out how to plan for the success of our vision.

What is a plan? By definition, a plan is a detailed proposal for doing or achieving something. It's an intention or decision about what one is going to do. It's important to understand that when we make a plan, we are putting action to the goals we have set. This is an energizing step in fulfilling your vision. Albert Einstein once said, "Nothing happens until something moves."[6] I want you to settle in your mind that your vision, goals, and confessions will not happen until you progress forward through a plan.

When you plan, you become intentional about your desires. You make them your aim, a part of your designed life, and they are interwoven into your purpose. At the end of the day, the entire process of vision is to get your life on the path to purpose, and that's exactly what a plan does. It's the moving parts behind what you see and speak. When we

6. Robert J. Ringer, *Action!: Nothing Happens Until Something Moves* (Lanham, MD: M. Evans, 2004) 14.

speak of plans, we are talking about the blueprints to our dreams. It's so important to realize the power of your goals when you have a plan. Plans break down the complex and make them simple and workable. The purpose of a vision is not the vision itself. It is not a pipe dream, that is to say, an unattainable or fanciful hope. The purpose of a vision is to see it come to pass. There are specific steps to planning for the success of your vision, and I will share them with you in this chapter.

> It's so important to realize the power of your goals when you have a plan. The purpose of a vision is not the vision itself. It is not a pipe dream, that is to say, an unattainable or fanciful hope. The purpose of a vision is to see it come to pass.

Even in my limited vision-writing abilities of my army days, plans were a natural part of the progression. I didn't have a clearly written vision, confession, or plan; yet everything I wrote came to pass. Why did it work when I had such limited knowledge of the process? I had only a list of goals but found tremendous success. It was because, on a deeper level, my goals created plans of action in my mind. I knew that if I wanted to reach my physical fitness goals, I had to put in extra work to accomplish them. I knew I would have to change my diet and be more mindful of my cravings and appetite for unhealthy food. I knew I had to run when everyone else was resting. I had to go the extra mile if I wanted to see my goals come to fruition. The amazing thing about it is that I exceeded my expectations with only a short list of goals. Internally, I was forming plans on how to accomplish them.

I have found that my goals are even more obtainable when I write out my plans. You see, when you write out a plan for your goals, you send a powerful message to your mind. You tell yourself that you intend to accomplish what you have dreamed and that you have charted a course for its completion. The interesting thing about a plan is that, just like your vision, it requires faith and filling in pieces to a puzzle that you may not yet have all the information for. You must see a solution where there is no solution. You must imagine a way when there is no way. That's what makes a plan so powerful. A plan creates opportunities for your success even when they are not apparent at the time of writing. You will find that your mind is geared toward strategies and that the plan-writing process, although challenging at first, is actually part of your mind's normal function. Your mind loves to make plans, and it does it on a continual basis, even when you're not conscious of it. That's why this process is so important, because you can employ your natural aptitude as a plan-maker in proactive, intentional ways.

Many people are products of their plan making. When they are not deliberate and clear about what they want in life, they fall to default responses. Their mind plans what they think about the most—whether good or bad. Our minds are a plan-making factory, constantly producing a product. When our minds aren't focused on our goals, we will produce plans unconsciously. If we think about our relationship problems, for instance, then our mind will set up plans to continually produce the same problems over and over. We are a product of what we give our time and attention to, nothing more and nothing less.

> If you are given to excessive worry, your mind will set up plans to produce what you are worrying about. This is a vicious cycle that can only be broken through deliberate vision writing, goal setting, confession, and planning.

If you are given to excessive worry, your mind will set up plans to produce what you are worrying about. This is a vicious cycle that can only be broken through deliberate vision writing, goal setting, confession, and planning. When you are focused on what you want instead of what you are currently experiencing, you are setting yourself up for a major breakthrough. The Bible clearly states that we are what we think about the most: *"For as he thinks in his heart, so is he"* (Proverbs 23:7

NKJV). What you think about is what you will become, and your mind will give you plans for its accomplishment. Now let's look at how we can focus our attention on our goals and write plans for what we want to happen in our lives.

The first step is to ask yourself what your objective is. What is the reason behind the why? Do you want a more stable living environment, a happier home life, and a more stable source of income? Look deep within and discover your real reasons for going after this goal. This is important because it cuts to the core of your motivation, and your motivation determines your ultimate outcome. You see, God responds to pure motive. He's not in the business of opening doors for people with wrong motives. Everything we do must at some level serve a higher purpose. This is why goal setting and dreaming alone will not produce results if we refuse consider the deeper issues of the heart. If you really want to be effective at writing plans, pay attention to this part of the process. God is much more interested in your development as a person and the formation of your character. When we stay on the surface level, we limit our capacity to tap into to the greatest attributes of God. Matthew 6:33 says, *"Seek ye first the kingdom of God, and his righteousness; and all these things shall be added unto you."* The reason questioning our motives is so important is because it's directly tied to our level of manifestation. God isn't going to bless you for just yourself. There is a far greater purpose for your blessing. It is to be shared with others and to give hope to the hurting and disillusioned. Ask yourself why you are wanting or doing this.

I remember when I asked myself this question. I wanted to know what my motivation was in ministry. First I said that it was to spread the gospel of Jesus Christ. This is certainly one of my reasons for doing this, but I knew there was something more. To help people perhaps? Yes, this is definitely why I do what I do, but there was something more. After much thought and soul-searching, it finally came to me: the main reason I do what I do is because it is truly my calling. I have never felt more alive, more like myself, more aware then when I'm doing what I truly love to do and feel called to do. That was it! My main objective or mission, if you will, was to do what God had designed me for and put me on this planet to do. That's where I started. I wrote down my plan for ministry at the top of a piece of paper. Then I wrote "mission" on the first line and penned this phrase: "My highest reason for doing ministry is to fulfill my calling and purpose doing what I love to do."

This is the essence of planning. Finding out why we do something will eventually reveal how we are going to do something. Many times, it will reveal that we need to adjust the why so we can have the how. If you are seeking something with a wrong motive, that is, to impress someone or to show someone up, then you have to find out if what you are seeking is really what you need. It's only out of pure desire with the greatest impact for good that we will see our dreams manifest. If we desire something with ill intent, then we are seeking the wrong things in life. Everything you seek should not only elevate your life but elevate the lives of everyone you meet. Look at your business or career goals and ask yourself why you want to accomplish them. If your goals are motivated by money or status, then you are not operating in your highest calling. When you are doing what you have been called to do, you will go to bed at night excited about waking up the next morning. I want you to live an exciting and thrilling life of adventure. I know that this can be accomplished only by living your life according to your calling.

The Latin root for vocation is *vox*, meaning "voice," and *vocare*, meaning "to call." So your vocation should be a voice calling you to fulfill your ultimate destiny. What would your life look like if you found and followed your true calling in life? You were placed here for a specific purpose, to do something meaningful not only for yourself but for all those connected to you. You can have a more meaningful experience in life if you find what's calling out for you. You may ask how to find the right calling and correct motives. As we discussed, this comes only from seeking God's plan for your life. Most people don't know their purpose and have no idea how to find it. I believe that your calling is directly linked to your connection. Your nexus with God determines the insight you have into what you have been called to do.

It's important to note that there are some other indicators that can help you find your calling. If something really bothers you and you feel compelled to do something about it, you may have found your calling. You will feel compelled to meet a need or fill a gap in society. Sometimes, you need only to look at your own life and the struggles of your past to find your calling. So many people have turned tragedy into triumph by helping other people get through what they went through. It's so important to know that your calling will always call you to a higher place of love, peace, and service to others. There is nothing more rewarding than to love what you do and do what you love. Even more rewarding is when what you do helps others.

> So many people have turned tragedy into triumph by helping other people get through what they went through. It's so important to know that your calling will always call you to a higher place of love, peace, and service to others.

The next step in writing out a plan for your goals is to set some more goals. I know this may sound counterintuitive, but I promise it's not. I used to write long-term goals and short-term goals until I discovered how to plan for the completion of my goals by taking action. My short-term goals were replaced with my plan. You see, I told you to dream your highest dream and write goals and affirmations for them, but now I'm going to show you how to hit smaller targets that will ultimately lead you to the fulfillment of your dreams.

I think many of us know the disappointment of making major New Year's resolutions only to fall back into the same old patterns of the year before. Where do the failures come in? The problem arises when we don't have small, more obtainable goals to motivate us along the way. After you have written out your mission statement or your highest reason for doing something, formulate smaller goals. I wrote down some things I wanted to happen along the way in my ministry. My first goal was to preach at the International Holy Convocation for the Church of God in Christ. I believed that this was a necessary step in the progression toward success in ministry. My second goal was to have speaking engagements every week. My third and final goal was to meet the presiding bishop. Now I had three goals to support my ultimate goal, which was success in ministry. I knew that if I accomplished these goals, I would accomplish my overall goal.

Notice that these goals would take tremendous faith and action to fulfill. Also understand that this caused great doubt and fear in me. It's important to understand that a real dream causes doubt to enter into your mind. A real dream makes you doubt that it can really happen. This is a natural part of the vision process, because you are attempting to break out of the box; your old mind-sets are stubborn and don't like change. You will find yourself questioning whether this can work. Perhaps you have failed in the past or are so consumed with the now that you can't possibly see how things could turn around for you. The amazing thing about a plan and smaller goals is that they can really change your life in relation to the failures of your past and the pull of where you currently are in life.

It's so important to take the time to think through these smaller supporting goals because they are the driving force behind your biggest dreams and aspirations. You may want to look at your relationship goals and what it will take to have a happy and fulling home life. What are some things that you could immediately begin to work on in your life? You may need to make marriage counseling a goal. You could write that you want to have one date night a week with your spouse. The ultimate goal is a great relationship, but the how to get there is found in smaller goals.

After you have written out your mission statement and your smaller goals, write down strategies for how you will accomplish them. This is where you take the action on the goals and move them to the next level of activity.

After you have written out your mission statement and your smaller goals, write down strategies for how you will accomplish them. This is where you take the action on the goals and move them to the next level of activity. Using the relationship model, we will formulate strategies. The question you must ask yourself is how you are going to make these goals a reality. What are you going to do right now that will put immediate action to what you have written down? A strategy for starting marriage counseling might be to Google search counselors in your area and call to set up an appointment. Your strategy for one date night a week may be to call a sitter and make reservations at your spouse's favorite restaurant. The key to a strategy is found in the immediate action you will take to accomplish your smaller goals, which will eventually feed the momentum of the major goal. Here's an example of how this would look when put all together.

Plan for a Relationship

Mission: To enjoy the family God has blessed me with and to live in harmony and happiness

Goals:

1. Start weekly marriage counseling.

2. Have one date night a week with my wife/husband.

3. Spend one hour a day reading to my child(ren).

Strategies:

1. Search the Internet for counselors in my area.

2. Call and make reservations at my wife/husband's favorite restaurant.

3. Buy or download children's books to read.

Do you see the pattern here and the power of a written plan? You literally go from the broad goal that was a derivative of the grand vision you wrote out, to a mission, then to smaller goals, and finally strategies on how to make it all happen. Suddenly, what seemed so far away when you first wrote your vision is broken down into actions you can immediately take toward reaching your ultimate goals. It's only when you break it all down that you get to the roots, which are the actions you can take right now to start down the path to fulfillment.

Here's another example related to health. Your goal may be to reach a certain target weight or to be healthier. It may look something like this:

Plan for a Healthy Lifestyle

Mission: To weigh the right amount for my body type and to live a heathy life

Goals:

1. Start an exercise regimen.

2. Eat healthier.

3. Count my calories.

Strategies:

1. Join a gym.

2. Stop eating sweets.

3. Download a calorie counter app.

Once again, we see the larger goal broken down into smaller goals and then the actions that will be taken to accomplish these goals. We see the timeless principle given by Mark Twain, "The secret of getting ahead is getting started. The secret of getting started is breaking your complex, overwhelming tasks into small manageable tasks, and then starting on the first one."[7] As you work with the plans of your life, you will see that what seems so distant and unmanageable suddenly looks like a doable task. You will see the complex become something you can

7. Mark Twain quoted in John Borek, Danny Lovett, and Elmer Towns, *The Good Book on Leadership: Case Studies from the Bible* (Nashville, TN: Broadman & Holman Publishers, 2005), 61.

start to immediately do as soon as your strategies are set. The key to the plan process is getting it to a place where you can actually *do* something. Remember the words of Einstein: "Nothing happens until something moves." You need movement and fluidity in your larger goals. You need targets, which are your smaller, short-term goals, and you need some things to do, which are your strategies.

One you start working your plan, you will begin to see things start lining up for you. I have written down certain things to do in my plan only to see more and even greater opportunities open up to me. The plan is something to get you moving, but once you start moving, the momentum kicks in and you begin to see a world of opportunities open to you. You will suddenly start to see the right people showing up in your life. You will see new paths to your goals. You will find favor with banks, employers, and clients.

> The plan is something to get you moving, but once you start moving, the momentum kicks in and you begin to see a world of opportunities open to you. You will suddenly start to see the right people showing up in your life. You will see new paths to your goals.

The plan is such an amazing tool because it gives your mind something to work with. Your brain loves to have a task or problem to work out. Unless you are deliberate about what you give your mind to work on, it will produce whatever is there by default. The worst thing you can do in the vision process is to fail to give your mind something to do. The mind will always work on your life either by design or by default. When it works by default, you are subject to the ebb and flow of whatever wave is currently in your life. This is almost always a negative tide. The way to turn the tide is to be deliberate in your plan of action. Write a mission statement so you clearly know why you are doing something in the first place. Next, you need smaller goals to keep you on track and motivated. Then you need the strategies to put it all into motion.

I believe that a plan is by far the most powerful part of the vision process because of the practicality of it. Writing a plan is as important as writing out every other aspect of your vision. You write out positive confessions so you will have something to say. Writing out your plan is so you will have something to do. There is a connection between the muscles and the brain. When a golfer practices a shot over and over, the mind becomes trained to perform that motion through muscle memory. When you write out your plan, there is a connection between your muscles and your mind, solidifying the words written on the page.

I use this powerful method for all aspects of my life. For example, if I'm having a hard time with something in my life, I'll write it out on a piece of paper in full detail. I'll allow myself to explore how I'm feeling about it, why I feel that way, and what I'm going to do about it. This has had an amazing impact on my life. I have dealt with issues from my childhood, bad relationships, embarrassing moments, fears, doubts, and so many other areas. When I write out these words on paper, I see the root of my problem and how I feel about it. Then I start to see how to change it and what action I need to take. The amazing thing about this process, particularly in the area of past pain, is that I always come to a place of respecting the situation. I'm thankful to God for it because I know that, in some way, it has to work for my good. (See Romans 8:28.) It's truly incredible what simply writing things out can do for you when you take the time to get alone and deal with the issues facing your life. I urge you to not only write out a plan, but the next time you feel a certain way that is affecting your progress, to take out a piece of paper and write down how you feel and what you want to see happen in your life. If you do, you will see extraordinary change in your life.

Recently I lost my stepdad. He and I had a very difficult relationship. I had glossed over the pain and heartache I had felt about how he treated me and the lack of love I had felt in my home my entire life. I didn't realize it, but I had become bitter, and the pain from my childhood was motivating me to do all I could to never be like him. This created a disdain and a pride in me when I would accomplish things and further separate myself from my family. It created an aura of distance and anger between me and my family members. They probably thought I was being arrogant or that I thought I was better than them. This wasn't the case; I just didn't want to be like them because I was hurt by the relationship between me and my stepdad, and I was jealous that everyone else in the family, along with his friends, got the better side of him.

I realized that this wasn't a healthy way to live my life and decided to do something about it. I made up my mind that I would face it head on, take all the emotions surrounding this situation, and feel the pain. I made up my mind that I wouldn't do what I had done in the past, pretending that I was good even though I wasn't. I was going to deal with this once and for all. I didn't know it at the time, but this would prove to be a difficult process; I discovered that at the core of the problems I was facing was this anger I felt for my stepdad. It wasn't easy, and it took a lot of work, but I overcame it. Interestingly enough, the final healing came as he was lying unresponsive in intensive care the night he passed away.

You see, my stepdad was a hard man. He had become much nicer as the years progressed, but he wasn't in tune with his emotions. He hadn't been raised that way. He'd contracted polio at the age of seven and was severely deformed by the disease. He'd learned to be tough, which had made him oblivious to self-reflection, and he lacked the self-awareness needed to make significant emotional connections with people. Everything was superficial, and he always acted as if everything was good even though it wasn't. He told me he loved me one time in my life, but he was drunk when he did it. He never showed any type of affection, and there were many deep issues and problems between us. We had no emotional connection, and I was made to feel inferior and in the way. I never felt wanted or accepted. There was always something wrong with me in his eyes, and this had a profound impact on me for years to come. I felt insecure and defensive. I would always project strength and appear that I was invincible, but sadly I was anything but that. I was fragile and making it through life with something to prove. I was wounded, hurt, and unable to form meaningful relationships. I faced all this and took the time to deal with the emotions, feelings, and reality of the situation.

One of the most powerful ways I dealt with this issue was using the writing-it-out technique. When I felt a certain way or was having a hard time, I would sit down with my notebook and pen and write it out in great detail. I would express and explain exactly how I was feeling. Sometimes, I would have an idea and find a path to changing the issue. Other times, I just let it all bleed out on the pages—going through the emotions of it all, feeling all the pain, and facing what I had previously ignored. Through this process, I slowly began to gain a new perspective. I started seeing things differently, understanding more, and seeing a clear path on what I needed to do to experience true and lasting healing from my childhood wounds. I came to a place of deep gratitude and appreciation for the pain. Through writing it out, I began to see a purpose behind it all. I understood that what had happened to me didn't have to happen, but since it had, I had a choice; I could either spend the rest of my days trying to change the unchangeable past, or I could use it. I could make it a part of my vision, a part of my purpose in life. I could help people deal with major issues of their life because of my experience.

Just as I had written out my vision, my goals, my confessions, and my plan, I wrote out my pain and found purpose. I'm happy to report that I got my final resolution that night alone with my stepdad. I didn't bother having this conversation with him when he was alive because I knew he wasn't emotionally ready to really hear me or understand where I was coming from. I knew that it wouldn't be effective and that I had to deal with it all within myself if change was going to come. On my way to the hospital, I realized I needed to take some time and be alone with him to tell him all the things I couldn't tell him while he was conscious.

I remember how difficult this was. Even though I knew he couldn't respond, I felt awkward talking to him because we had never had this conversation before. Yet I knew it had to be done. I didn't recall everything he had done to me; in fact, I just gave a general overview that was encapsulated by my emotions and feelings more than specific events. I was able to do this because I had already dealt with all of that in my time of writing out how I felt about the specifics. When I started talking to him, he started moving around and it really seemed like he wanted to talk to me. I felt as if he was saying sorry by his movements. You may think I'm stretching this story and trying to make it out to be more than what it really was. Consider this, before I got there, he hadn't moved at all. Not until I started talking did he start moving. As he became more restless and seemingly agitated, I spoke softly in his ear and told him that I forgave him. I told him to rest easy and that everything was okay. I understood that I was now at peace, and I wanted him to be at peace. After I said this, his monitors started to go off, and I noticed a spike in his heart rate. The nurse came in and said that after a week in the hospital and days of being unconscious, he was now reading a fatal heart rate and that it wouldn't be long until he would pass away. It was as if he was waiting for me to get there and make peace with him. What we couldn't resolve all those years was resolved in the last hours of his time on earth.

This tremendous time of healing spilled over into my other relationship with other family members, toward whom I carried anger because they had all had a better relationship with him. After releasing my stepdad, I felt love and compassion toward my mom and my stepsisters. Through this experience, we all bonded and became close. It was as if he had done in death what he hadn't been able to do in life. I was only able to come to this point because I had written down my pain and my feelings and dealt with them on a deeper, more intimate level.

The point I want to make now is this: the reason you need a vision and plan for your life is because you don't want to be like my stepdad. Don't wait until death to live. In his final hours of unresponsiveness came the greatest amount of healing in my life and in the life of my family. I don't want you to wait until the end of your life to get the healing you can have right here, right now. I want you to dream the highest dream you can, pursue it with passion, and see your days filled with joy and fulfilment. You get only one chance to do this part of your life, so don't waste it on unforgiveness and a life of hurt and disappointment. If you have to write out your feelings every day until something changes, do it. Just as you can write your plans for your future, you can write out your emotions and wounds and receive healing and instruction on how to change.

I want you to dream the highest dream you can, pursue it with passion, and see your days filled with joy and fulfilment. You get only one chance to do this part of your life, so don't waste it on unforgiveness and a life of hurt and disappointment.

In this chapter, we learned how to take the grand vision of our future and put it into a workable model with which we can take action. The planning portion of the vision process is so important because it gives you what to do. It frees you from sitting around waiting for something to happen and shows you how to actually do something about it. It's time to take action, and your plan gives you the necessary tools to do so. I think the greatest challenge to planning is formulating what to do, because most of us don't know what that should look like. Thankfully, this part of the vision process isn't up to you. God already knows the path for you. As you take the time to write it out, He will give you the instructions on how to do it. It is really an act of faith to write out a plan because you will see things revealed to you that you may not have seen before. You will be required to do things that seem out of the ordinary, but if you do it, it will yield tremendous results. All you really need to do is be prayerful and open about what to write in your plan. This is key because God already has plans for you and will reveal them to you if you're willing to take action and write them out. Jeremiah 29:11 (NIV) says, "For I know the plans I have for you,' declares the LORD, 'plans to prosper you and not to harm you, plans to give you hope and a future.'" God has plans for every aspect of your life, and if you approach this part of your vision prayerfully and with this in mind, then God will reveal those plans to you.

Isn't so refreshing to know that God has an incredible plan for your life just waiting to unfold before you? You don't have to live a mundane existence. You can live a life of adventure, doing and being all God has created you to be. You can be prosperous, healthy, full of life, and able to serve others. You can truly live a life of abundance in your relationship with God, your family, other people in your everyday experience. Happiness, love, and security aren't just things of fantasy. They are real and promised to you in God's Word. As you seek God for the plans He has for your life, you will prosper and have hope for the future. God doesn't want you to walk around in fear and anxiety about the future. He wants you to be excited about every day and enjoy the life He has so richly blessed you with. Take the next step and write out a plan for your goals so you can take action today, right now. Time is passing, and you can't go back to yesterday. Make the most of what you have, which is right now.

NOTHING TO FEAR

SEVEN

NOTHING TO FEAR

One thing I have noticed when I start to dream is that fear always creeps in. No matter how much I safeguard against it or try to avoid this part of the vision process, it is always there. When you challenge the norms of your life and dare to see something different than what you have been experiencing up to that point, you will experience uncomfortable challenges. You see, I believe that we become comfortable with where we are because it has become normal. To challenge that brings doubt, and the root of doubt is fear. I want to share with you what the Bible says about fear and how to deal with it when it comes because, believe me, when you start to dream, it will come in many forms. You don't have to be subject to its emotional ebbs and flows; you can defeat it and see your dreams come to pass.

There is a very common acronym for fear: false evidence appearing real. I want you to understand that there is a place for fear, and it serves a purpose in your protection. This, however, isn't the fear I'm talking about. The fear I'm talking about wraps its hands around your potential and tells you all the reasons why you can't do something. It's a debilitating fear of the unknown and how you will be able to navigate the dreams and visions that are coming your way. Fear presents evidence, but that evidence isn't true. When I was preparing to go into basic training, I was given a valuable nugget of advice. I was told that you can't properly prepare yourself for what is coming because things are never as you think they will be. I believe that we can write out our dreams and that God will bring them to pass. I believe that you can imagine what that will look like and prepare for it. This certainly applies to fear.

Fear tries to set up a scenario in your mind. Fear shows you a picture of unsuccessfulness and failure. If you're not careful, you will allow these false images to become so real that they become a self-fulfilling prophecy. If you allow fear to tell you that you will never get out of debt, you will never be healed, you will die, or you will never break an addiction, then you will do so. You will become the most dominate thought in your life. You will find yourself becoming what you are afraid of. I have often heard it said that fear and faith can't cohabitate. I agree on one hand because, at some point, fear has to give way to faith in order for manifestation to take place. I also believe that fear is a natural response to faith. I believe that faith produces a certain level of fear because you doubt whether or not what you dreamed can actually happen. You also disrupt your current level of security because you have to step out of your comfort zone to experience what you are believing for. So the question is, how do we deal with the inevitable fear that will come when we allow ourselves to dream? In my experience, the most effective way is to do what we discussed in the chapter on confessions. We have to find out what the Bible says about fear and apply it to our life.

Fear is a natural response to faith. I believe that faith produces a certain level of fear because you doubt whether or not what you dreamed can actually happen. You also disrupt your current level of security because you have to step out of your comfort zone to experience what you are believing for.

Before we deal with how to eradicate fear, let's define what fear really is, what we need to know about it, and the multitude of anxieties and confusions that come along with it. Unfortunately, fear is our default response that is born with us into this world. The cause of this inborn fear comes from a feeling of separation and loneliness. Every person on this planet is born with a sense of disconnection. In fact, our very first experience in the earth realm is just that, separation. We have to leave the comfort of our mother's womb. We are torn away from a place of security and warmth, where the very hand of God formed and developed us. When we are born, we are brought from a security into a place of harsh reality. The first world we leave is the awesome heavenly realm of our loving God. The second world is the soothing place of the womb in which we are developed. It's no wonder that children's first response to their new environment is to cry. They have left two beautifully comforting places to encounter the physical and emotional elements of the outside world.

It's important to note that this process of external anxiety can occur while still in the womb. Studies have shown that the emotional state of the mother can significantly affect the fetus. Growing older, I discovered that I felt very rejected and unwanted. At first, I thought this was because of my relationship with my stepfather and the feeling that my mom had left me to him and didn't intervene. I also felt as if my sister, who was their child together, got the love I had always craved and desired. I was told my entire life that my real father was the man my mother was married to when she became pregnant with me. She'd told me that he didn't want anything to do with me. This only enhanced my feelings of rejection.

Later on, I found out the truth. I discovered that my mother had been raped and that I was the product. After researching several pre-natal psychology, I come to understand that even though my mother decided to keep me after much internal debate, I had already experienced the same rush of emotion from her that she was now dealing with. I was bathed in rejection from my mother's womb because I was the epitome of an unwanted pregnancy. So even before I got here, I was dealing with rejection. Even in the comfort of what is supposed to be a safe and beautiful environment, the elements of the outside world can still have an impact. This world needless to say is a wakeup call when we enter it and studies show that this can begin before we ever get here.

Regardless of the circumstances of your birth, we all come in "crying" because we are separated from comfort for the first time. This separation, of course, predates us and has its origin in the Genesis narrative. Adam and Eve were never born out of the womb. They were created for all intents and purposes as adults. Adam was formed from the dust of the ground, and God Himself breathed life into him. His wife, Eve, was formed from his rib, and they never knew separation from God. They were created and placed in a beautiful paradise with the promise of expanding heaven on earth through procreation. Before the fall of man, even childbirth was to be a glorious and beautiful ordeal. All of that changed, of course, when Adam and Eve succumbed to the serpent's cunning tactics. The ultimate separation from God came during man's fall from grace in the garden of Eden, and since that time, we all have had to contend with separation.

At times, we all have felt disconnected from God and from the people around us. This can cause us to be depressed and filled with anxiety. In fact, I believe that the real cause of anxiety is the feeling of separation. When we feel disconnected from God, we want to feel reconnected. If we don't know how to do this, we try to control these feelings. It is impossible to control separation with reconnection; when we try, we feel out of control and fear creeps in. We were never created to be in control. We were created to be under control, to be under the influence of God's divine love, protection, grace, and comfort. Without this connection, we feel hopeless, powerless, and afraid. This is not the will of God for our lives. We were not created to live in fear and anxiety; we were created to feel the love and connection to the all-powerful Master of the universe.

We were never created to be in control. We were created to be under control, to be under the influence of God's divine love, protection, grace, and comfort. Without this connection, we feel hopeless, powerless, and afraid. This is not the will of God for our lives.

In the rest of this book, I will endeavor to take you beyond the physical realm of the vision process and show you that God wants to see you prosper and to be healthy and to see your soul prosper. He wants to bring you into a deeper, more meaningful relationship with Him. If you make Him your focus, everything else you desire will begin to show up in your life. Faith is certainly a force for bringing the spiritual world into the natural world, but this is most easily accomplished when you are connected to a loving and compassionate God. When you reestablish this nexus with His love, you will find that all your desires are attached to it. Jesus said, "*Seek ye first the kingdom of God, and his righteousness; and all these things shall be added unto you*" (Matthew 6:33). As we seek to know Him on a deeper, more visceral level, we will see the importance of a truly connected life and the spiritual and natural benefits of seeking Him first.

Many times, we allow the cares and distractions of this life to get in the way of what really matters. It's like a man who stays at home with his children but is more in tune with what's on the television than with forming a bond with his kids. He's there in in person but not in mind. He even yells at the kids to be quiet, so he can ignore them even more. Just as this man wastes precious time with his kids that he can never get back, so, too, we waste precious time concerned about what and how we are going to get what we want. When we turn off the distractions and really seek to know God, everything else will fall in place.

The only way to truly deal with fear is to deal with separation anxiety, because when we are connected to God, fear dissipates and the joy of connection and fulfilment returns. I want you to know that you are not alone. I know that you may feel like that. You may even feel as if there is no one you can trust or talk to—but you need to know that God is there all the time. Deuteronomy 31:6 says that God will not fail or forsake us. He is always standing by waiting on you to come to Him and to be at peace.

Let's take a look at some verses that will help you deal with this issue of fear related to separation and find victory over it. First John 4:18 says, *"There is no fear in love; but perfect love casteth out fear: because fear hath torment. He that feareth is not made perfect in love."* In this verse, we see an incredible connection between love and fear. You wouldn't think that these have anything to do with each other until you look a little deeper and see that they are interactively tied to each another. The preceding verses talk about how God sent His son Jesus Christ into the world and that when we confess Him as our Lord, He will dwell in us. Because God is the most perfect and pure form of love that can be experienced, when He enters us, we can experience this type of eternal and overwhelming love in our lives and extend that love to others. John goes on to say that our bond with God is a bond of love. He tells us that when we experience God, we both know and believe the love that God has for us. In other words, this is experiential love, not just theoretical love. This is real love that comes from a God encounter. John tells us that God is love. His very nature and essence is pure, unconditional love. What a refreshing thought in a world that can seem so hostile—we have a God that is all in all pure love. If you take a moment to dwell on that thought, then perhaps your perception of God will change.

I have found that there are a lot of people who think otherwise of God. When I would get hurt as a child, a neighbor would say, "That's God getting you back." It was if he was saying that God was in the business of payback. Many of us either consciously or subconsciously see or have seen God as this type of cruel person. This is not God at all. God wants to see you happy and joyful, not living in fear that you are on the verge of losing His love if you make a mistake. On the contrary, the Bible teaches that God is a forgiving God: *"If we confess our sins, he is faithful and just to forgive us our sins, and to cleanse us from all unrighteousness"* (1 John 1:9).

Many times, we blame God for the things that have happened to us and, therefore, see Him as a cruel and unfair God. The reason that the vision process is so important is because it reveals the truth. You see, God has given you free will. You have the right to choose Him, and you have the right to either come in line with His purpose for your life or not. Most of us chose not to, not because we are rebellious or trying to go off course, but simply because we don't know what that purpose is or how to break out of our current situation. Therefore, we blame God for how our life has turned out, when He is saying, "I have a glorious life just waiting for you if you can get in contact with Me."

When I was in the army, I remember talking with another soldier about God. He viewed God as a punisher, and he even seemed to take pride in his understanding of God liking to get people for doing wrong. Now, I'm not suggesting that there aren't consequences for your actions, but God's intent is not to punish you for everything you do wrong. He is a loving and compassionate God who wants to heal and restore your soul.

> God's intent is not to punish you for everything you do wrong. He is a loving and compassionate God who wants to heal and restore your soul.

John goes on to say that the person who dwells in love dwells in God and that God dwells in him. (See 1 John 4:16.) The word *"dwell"* in translated from the Greek word *meno,* which means to stay (in a given place, state, relation, or expectancy), abide, continue, dwell, endure, remain, or be present. I want to draw your attention to the phrase "be present." I believe that this carries such a powerful explanation of what dwelling in love actually means. We spoke earlier about speaking our confessions in the now, as if we already had them, and I want to take that even further here.

You see, we think of time in a linear way, but it is nonlinear. God is an eternal now, which means that everything is happening in the present. This is especially difficult for us to understand because our minds think in terms of beginning and end. We are most comfortable thinking in terms of the past and the future. Many times, we let the only thing we truly have, now, to slip away. Amazingly, we struggle with this concept, with the place that God resides. Everything past and present is fully expressed in the now, eternal aspect of who God is. So, when we dwell in love, we are to take the thoughts of the past and present and bring them into the abiding place of God's love for us now.

This is particularly important if you have a troubled past. You cannot change what has happened in your life. Perhaps you were mistreated, were done wrong, or made mistakes. The point is, you can't go back and change that part of your life, but you can choose how it will affect you. You can either carry the pain of it with you for the rest of your life, or you can drown it in the ever present, eternal, and abiding love of God. I want you to try something right now. Take the worst time of your life, the place of your greatest dis-appointment or pain, and change the way you look at it. Thank God for the unpleasant event and find a place of deep gratitude. Don't allow it to take you to a place of anger or strife; rest in the fact that love conquers all.

I had to do this recently when my dad died. I had to surround this place of pain and rejection with love. I realized that what happened to me didn't have to happen, but it did. I understood that I could take that pain and somehow make it work for me, that I could be empow-ered by my past if I could find a way to cover it with love. Isn't that the essence of what love does? It has the incredible ability to cover you and all you have done. Look at what Peter said: *"Most important of all, con-tinue to show deep love for each other, for love covers a multitude of sins"* (1 Peter 4:8 NLT). Deep, compassionate love covers a multitude of sins.

"*Covers*" in this verse means to hide, to veil, to hinder the knowledge of a thing. "*Sins*" means offenses. So love has the power to hide people's offenses. This is an awesome idea when you think of all the people you have hurt in your life, but it's even more impactful when you think of all the people who may have hurt you. Once again, the antidote for pain and offense is the all-consuming love of God dwelling in our hearts.

John continues to say that if we dwell in love, then we dwell in God and God dwells in us. (See 1 John 4:16.) Then he says that this love gives us boldness because as Jesus was in this world, so are we in this world. (See 1 John 4:17.) In other words, through love we understand that we are just temporary residents here, but we have an awesome responsibility to share this love with everyone we encounter while we are here. What would our world look like if we could escape our self-loathing long enough to share the love of Christ with the people around us? We have daily encounters with people who are hurting, disillusioned, and lost. What comfort we could bring. What joy we could give if we understood first the love by which God loves us and the love we could share with others.

I'm not suggesting that this is an easy endeavor; the truth is we are at great risk when we love. Love can be rejected and mistreated and can put us in a seemingly precarious position. The truth, however, is that it doesn't matter what others do with the love we extend because when we operate in love, we fulfill our ultimate purpose on the earth and the reward of joy and fulfilment is secured for us. Jesus put it this way: "*A new command I give you: Love one another. As I have loved you, so you must love one another*" (John 13:34 NIV).

Now we get to the crux of the teaching "*There is no fear in love; but perfect love casteth out fear: because fear hath torment. He that feareth is not made perfect in love*" (1 John 4:18). The antidote for the separation anxiety we feel is love. The cure for the fear of being disconnected from God is love. We have learned that to be in love is to dwell in God and for God to dwell in you. This verse explicitly states that fear and love are opposing ideas and can't coexist. So when we are overtaken by fear and overrun with anxiety, we have only one place to turn. We are to come back to that place of pure, unconditional love that comes only from God. This verse goes on to say, *"Perfect love casteth out fear."* *"Perfect"* in this verse means to be complete. So complete love can cast out fear. We have to come to a place of connection in prayer and in the abiding truths of God's Word to reestablish our relationship of love with God.

Let's be honest, most of us don't spend quality daily time in prayer. Our lives have become so busy that we have edged God right out of our daily experience. What price do we pay? Our love grows cold because we haven't strengthened the bond with the divine. To be perfected in love, we have to spend time engulfed and submerged in the presence of an almighty and loving God. We must remove the rust of our relationship and put Him first again in our lives. When we do this, we will experience His perfect love and be complete in that love. We will find that this type of love casts fear out. *"Cast"* in this verse is translated from the Greek word *ballo,* which means "to throw or let go of a thing not caring where it falls." What an exhilarating thought! Can you imagine coming to a place where you truly let go of everything holding you back? Can you envision being in a place where you drop all your cares, fears, and doubts and you don't even care where they land? How do you come to this place? It comes through love, a love that is confident in and that trusts that God has control of your life. This is that place of knowing that everything is in His hands and nothing can get to you unless it first goes through Him.

What are you holding on to? What are you afraid of? What is holding you back? Whatever it is, you can overcome it, and you can be made whole again. You can be completely and totally restored. It's all found in the love of God. Take a risk today and step into His love. You've tried to fix it, you've tried to work it, and it has only gotten worse. Accept God's love for you today, and allow it to cast off fear. The end of 1 John 4:18 says, *"He that feareth is not made perfect in love."* That's it right there! That's your answer! The only way things are going to change for you, the only way you can overcome the doubts and fears about your vision, is to be completely in love with God and to allow His love to surround every fiber of your being. He loves you, and He wants you to be free from what you are carrying around. It's through love that fear goes!

> The only way things are going to change for you, the only way you can overcome the doubts and fears about your vision, is to be completely in love with God and to allow His love to surround every fiber of your being. He loves you, and He wants you to be free from what you are carrying around.

We see the connection between love and fear in another Scripture. Timothy tells us, *"For God has not given us the spirit of fear, but of power and of love and of a sound mind"* (2 Timothy 1:7 NKJV). This verse tells us that unhealthy fear about life, health, and our future is not a part of the Spirit of God. The Greek word for *"spirit"* here is *pneuma*, which deals with man's spirit and God's spirit. It means "breath," like that initial breath breathed into Adam's nostrils by God. It deals with the rational soul and the spirit of the divine. This is an amazing concept because in all our scientific endeavors as a species, the one thing researchers and scientists can't explain is where consciousness comes from. They can pinpoint all the different functions of the brain, but they are completely dumbfounded on this portion of the mind. The reason they can't understand it is because it is not of this world. It is the spirit, the soul of a person, which is not of this world. The mind is part of the body and helps the body function, but the spirit is otherworldly. It is in the realm of the unseen. In this verse, God tells us that the spirit He gives us is not one of fear.

Fear comes from outside this space. It comes from the many vicissitudes of life and our perception of what we think will or will not happen. When we feed our spirits on God's Spirit, we are no longer subject to the natural course of things. We are now in contact with a supernatural force that is beyond the limitations of this earthly experience. All things become possible when we make this transition.

"*Fear*" in this verse isn't translated from the Greek word *phobia*, which we normally see. Instead, it is translated from the word *deilia*, which means "timidity, fearfulness, and cowardice." So, in essence, Timothy is conveying to us that God isn't the author of cowardice but that, through the power of His Spirit, He will strengthen our spirit to be able to face and overcome any obstacle that comes our way. John speaks to this point when he says, "*Greater is he that is in you, than he that is in the world*" (1 John 4:4). When we feel the inevitable doubt and fear that arise when we dare to dream our highest dream, when we write out our goals with boldness, when we confess with confidence that what we believe will happen, and when we write out our plans, we should pull upon the strength of this verse. We can boldly declare that we are not cowards. God hasn't given us that spirit; we have a spirit of power, love, and a sound mind. (See 2 Timothy 1:7.)

Isn't it amazing that love is a recurring theme when dealing with fear? God gives us power and soundness of mind, and it all works through the device of love. Love is not only the key to overcoming fear but the key to manifesting our desires. Everything God did in creating this world was out of an abundance of love. If you're going to create a better life for yourself, it will come through love. In fact, your faith works only when mixed with love. Galatians 5:6 (AKJV) says, "*Faith which works by love.*"

I have seen so many frustrated believers because they have stopped believing. Their belief in God hasn't ceased, but their belief in what God can and will do in their life has. They have become weak in faith. When they prayed, they felt as if their prayer would not be answered, and over time, they just gave up on hope for a better future. Many times, an examination of their life will show a disconnect with God in prayer. This disconnect creates a chasm between them and the love of God. This lack of felt love from the Creator through neglect of the relationship causes them to weaken. When this love is affected, their relationships with others are affected. They no longer share from the abundance of God's love because their own reserves are depleted.

The answer is found in reestablishing their connection with God. From this place, we are able to find His abundant love for us, which overflows to others. When our love is working, it becomes the conduit to our faith. We have just learned that faith works by love. This means that access to the unseen realm, where perfect love abides, comes by way of love. Love comes through a connection with God, which we nurture on a daily basis. The more we bathe in love and express that love for others, the more we cast off the chains of fear and are enabled to access our vision by faith. It is a fallacy to teach strictly on faith and not on love because we all came from a spirit realm of complete and total love, and we all will return there again someday. Faith can be rendered effective only when it is used with love. It is this divine language of love that is spoken in eternity and must be the spoken our hearts should we gain access to this realm.

> Faith can be rendered effective only when it is used with love. It is this divine language of love that is spoken in eternity and must be the spoken our hearts should we gain access to this realm.

If you an American traveling to France, you are placing yourself in a different environment. The French language and culture are very different. I have been to Paris and have absolutely loved it. One of the complaints about French people that I hear from Americans is that they are rude. I had a completely different experience. It's not that they are rude, it's that their cultural responses and norms are different. I'm from Alabama, where we have a different way of speaking. Sometimes, we speak to others with a head nod or, when driving, with a slight wave to people in the car or those on the street. This, of course, is not the norm in New York City and Paris. If someone doesn't speak to me in a way I'm used to, it's not rude; it's just different.

The other complaint from many Americans about France is that the portions of food are too small. In my opinion, France has the best food I have ever put in my mouth from anywhere in the world. It's interesting to note that the French eat foods higher in fat and cholesterol. They smoke and drink more than Americans, yet they have a longer life span. Why? Because of portion control. They eat more fatty foods but smaller portions. They savor every bite instead of scarfing down loads of food at a buffet and bringing a doggie bag to go. Their portions are smaller not to keep them from being full but so they can savor every bite and enjoy the food.

We see this same concept when dealing with the spiritual realm. It has a specific culture and language. The culture is dominated by love and compassion. The language of heaven, whether spoken or unspoken, is a language of all-encompassing love. Just as if you were in France, the more you learn the language and the culture of the spirit, the more you will enjoy and be able to access it by faith. Your faith will come alive when you learn the language of love. You don't have to wait to adopt someone in a remote village to start speaking this language. You can begin with those in your home, the people in the house next door to you, or your coworkers. Make an attempt to connect with God's love in your life and share that with everyone you meet. As you do, it will expand, and so will your vision and the ability to manifest it.

So many times, I have heard teaching on faith that comes off as self-centered because the well-intentioned teacher is trying to expand to teach that we serve a limitless God, and this is so true. God really does want to bless us beyond our imagination. Psalm 84:11 says, *"For the LORD God is a sun and shield: the LORD will give grace and glory: no good thing will he withhold from them that walk uprightly."* God wants to tremendously bless us, but anything done in a spirit other than love and not in line with the principles of the heavenly realm will never come to pass. God isn't in the practice of allowing you to access your desires for your own glory. That's not to say that you won't get what you want—many people have been motivated by the wrong things and succeeded in getting what they wanted only to be disappointed and unfulfilled by the very thing they thought would bring them joy. You see, this thing is bigger than us. Only when we come from a perspective of expansive thinking that asks, "What can I do and be that will not only enhance my life but also the lives of others?" will we begin to see things work in our favor. True fulfillment, I have found, comes with care and concern for others in your endeavors.

> This thing is bigger than us. Only when we come from a perspective of expansive thinking that asks, "What can I do and be that will not only enhance my life but also the lives of others?" will we begin to see things work in our favor.

My wife loves to cook big dinners around the holidays. She is an incredible cook and finds great joy this time of the year. I watch her work feverishly to complete every task, sometimes cooking up to the point of people's arrival. Then I watch her serve others; generally, she is the last one to eat. I asked her one time how she did this. She said the joy is in watching people eat what she has created. This is the essence of the manifestation process. God wants to see you enjoy what you have prayed for, but He equally wants you to know the joy of seeing others blessed by what He has done for you. This is one of the ways we can share this incredible love. God loves us so much that He even takes care of those who don't acknowledge Him.

Once Jesus was speaking about our need to forgive others, to pray for our enemies, and to salute those who don't like us. He said that if we do this, we will be like our Father in heaven. Matthew 5:45 (NIV) puts it this way: "He causes his sun to rise on the evil and the good, and sends rain on the righteous and the unrighteous." This is a powerful truth that tells us, just like God, our love should extend to all created beings because, in the end, this world is held together by love. If we are to change any aspect of our lives, it must be accomplished by and through the guise of pure love for God and our fellow man. Love for God, love for the life He has blessed us to live, and love for all life is the key to a happy, healthy, and fulfilling life.

As we discussed earlier, our fears come from feelings of separateness, that inevitable anxiety that comes from feeling alone in the world. This feeling can only be nullified when we establish and maintain our relationship with our all-loving Creator. Isaiah 41:10 speaks to this point when he said, *"Fear thou not; for I am with thee: be not dismayed; for I am thy God: I will strengthen thee; yea, I will uphold thee; yea, I will uphold thee with the right hand of my righteousness."* Notice how distinct and straightforward this verse begins. It states emphatically, *"Fear thou not."* Is this the way to do it? Just simply make a decision that you won't fear? Of course, that's not the implication here because the verse goes on to explain why you don't have to fear. You see, to tell a person struggling with anxiety that they need to stop being anxious because Philippians 4:6 (NIV) says, *"Do not be anxious"* is futile. Fear is inculcated in the hearts of us all because of the separation we feel at birth from our Creator. There is no quick fix to fear. Then you add all the reasons we should fear: terrorism reports, strains of bacteria immune to antibiotics, multiple senseless deaths on a daily basis, kidnappings, theft, and the list goes on.

We are bombarded with images and sounds that tell us to fear. Fear has become a part of our culture and is often used as a method by salespeople. The concept is called fear and consumption. I have seen many pastors and leaders use this tactic at conferences I attend. Once I heard a presentation from a lawyer who specialized in tax law for nonprofit organizations. He scared everyone in the room by reeling off statistics of all the pastors and staff members who had gone to jail, and he promised to keep us all from the same fate. We all should be good stewards of God's money, but some haven't been; this shouldn't have been the selling point of his presentation. However, this man understood that fear brings consumption; sure enough, pastors were lined up at his table to become his clients.

Fear, then, is not only real but is inflated by many people. The local nightly news reports on all the bad things that have happened in your area and in the world. People are so captivated by it that they tune in to hear about all the murders, accidents, and fires. Then they are bombarded with commercials of products to soothe their fears. I'm not against the news—I think it is important to stay informed—but I am limited on what I can do to prevent or thwart what's taking place on a daily basis. The only thing I can do is take responsibility for my actions and my thought life. This is the key to dealing with fears. Things aren't ever going to change by simply stating that you will not fear. This is akin to putting a bandage on an infected wound without treating the wound. The bandage will only serve to further the infection. No, we must look deep within and at God's Word to find truths to change our minds. An overly fearful person has a storehouse of fearful thoughts. It's only when we work to change those thoughts that we can obey this Isaiah 41:10: *"Fear thou not."*

Isaiah 41:10 is so powerful because it tells us why we shouldn't fear. The first reason it gives is, *"I am with thee."* Just as we have discussed before, so many of us feel alone. We feel isolated, misunderstood, and separate. How can this be possible with so many people around us at all times? This isolation comes because we have lost our connection with the only One who matters—the One though whom all relationships should flow through. God is telling us that the main reason we have nothing to fear is because He is here with us right now. He was here before we were created, He is here through every step of our lives, and He will be there for us when we leave our bodies.

What a comforting thought to know that no matter where we are or where we go, we always have our loving Father with us every step of the way. It's important to understand this—to know that we are not alone that that God is there every step of the way—when we are bold enough to step out on our vision. When fear arises or that old voice of doubt begins to speak to us and tell us that it will never work, we can remind that voice that God is always with us. He is ever present and will always by our sides. One Greek terms for Holy Spirit means "one who walks beside." God walks through every difficulty in our life with us and ultimately guides us to the fulfillment of our dreams. Fear not, because He is with you every step of the way. (See Isaiah 41:10.) He will lead you and guide you into the best possible scenario for you, your family, and all those you have met or will meet in the future.

> When fear arises or that old voice of doubt begins to speak to us and tell us that it will never work, we can remind that voice that God is always with us. He is ever present and will always by our sides.

The next instruction is, *"Be not dismayed."* Once again, willpower alone can't make this happen. You can't will yourself into avoiding being dismayed. There has to be a reason why you're not dismayed and steps that you can take to ensure that. *"Dismayed"* in this verse is translated from the Hebrew word *sha'ah*, which means to "gaze about in anxiety." When you are dismayed, you are fixating your eyes and thus your attention on the object of trouble that is before you. It's interesting that this word carries the added weight of anxiety with it. You are fixated on the thing that causes you anxiety. The object of your fear holds your attention. When you are dismayed, you are looking at the wrong things.

It's so easy to fall into the trap of looking at the negative things in our lives. For many of us, that's all we've ever known and all we ever expect to see. That's why we have to shift our thinking, taking our focus off the wrong things. The Bible says, *"Looking unto Jesus the author and finisher of our faith"* (Hebrews 12:2). We have looked at and been dismayed by the pain of our past, the dire need of our present, and the bleak hope of a better future. We live on a reactionary level. We react to what comes our way, bracing for the next wave to hit us and shatter us again. It becomes a vicious cycle that we can't seem to break no matter how hard we try. Is there a cure for this malady, help for this pain, an end to the continual bad seasons of life? The answer is yes! We have to take our eyes off what has been happening and put our eyes on Jesus. We have to look to Him and His eternal Word for the answers that can create a new experience for us in this life.

Isaiah tells us that the antidote for feeling dismayed and continually gazing on the things that cause us anxiety is one powerful truth: "*I am thy God*" (Isaiah 41:10). This is the beginning of moving out of a fear-centered experience and living a real and happy existence. You have to know that He is your God. Look at the actual words Isaiah uses here. He says, "*I am.*" This is such an incredible statement. I Am is the name God revealed to Moses when he returned to Egypt to liberate the Hebrews from slavery. God told him, "*I Am That I Am*" (Exodus 3:14). I admit that this comes across as a mystical name and is somewhat difficult to understand. God was saying that He is an ever present, all-powerful God; that He was, and is, and would forever be with them.

He's saying the same thing to us. We don't have to fear or be dismayed because He was, is, and always will be with us. He is our eternal God. That's why He says, "*I am thy God.*" God makes His relationship personal. He's saying, "I've always been here for you, I'm here right now, and I'm never going to leave you." When you can resign to this fact in your mind, you will see anxiety and fear dissipate. You should practice saying this over and over to yourself: "My God is always right here for me. 'I Am' is my God; I have nothing to fear and my anxiety must go, because the living God is with me at all times."

Isaiah 41:10 (NIV) goes on to further solidify this thought, saying, "*I will strengthen you and help you; I will uphold you.*" We don't have to live our lives in doubt, fear, and torment anymore. We can trust that God is here to strengthen us when we are weak. He will help us through anything and everything, and He will keep us lifted up and moving forward regardless of what we face. Psalm 46:1 (ESV) puts it this way: *"God is our refuge and strength, a very present help in trouble."* I want you to know that you have nothing to fear in life. God is with you, He's for you, and He knows exactly what to do to make sure you make it through what you're dealing with right now and that you have the faith to live an even better tomorrow.

The last verse on fear I will share is Psalm 34:4, which says, *"I sought the LORD, and he heard me, and delivered me from all my fears."* David was talking about a time when, in a state of great fear and anxiety, he had been brought before King Abimelech, so he'd acted crazy in an attempt to keep himself from looking like a threat. It'd worked. When David scratched the walls and drooled down his beard, King Abimelech thought he was a madman and let him go. This seems like a favorable end, but there was a problem. David didn't trust in the Lord for this deliverance from the king, and he let his fear drive him to act this way. Most theologians date this psalm toward the end of David's life, when he was an older man reflecting on this event. It begins, *"I will bless the LORD at all times: his praise shall continually be in my mouth"* (Psalm 34:1). David was saying that he had made a mistake back then, that he had allowed fear to guide him and had acted like a madman because of it. He admitted that what he should have done was lift up his hands and do what we all should do regardless of the circumstances: *"Bless the LORD at all times."*

We can see that David learned a lesson. One of the most powerful ways to overcome fear is through praise and worship of God. As we learn to worship our way through the hardships of life, we will find unspeakable joy and comfort that far outweigh our fears. Worship and praise are so incredible because they can bring us into God's presence. When we come into God's presence, we are translated from the mundane to the miraculous. We don't have to be overcome by fear; we can worship until His presence overcomes and overwhelms us. The next time fear and anxiety come into your heart and mind, try taking David's advice and begin to worship and praise God. When you do, you will see a radical change from fear to faith—faith that is birthed out of the pure presence of the living God.

CHALLENGES TO VISION

EIGHT

CHALLENGES TO VISION

The Challenge of Time

I wish I could tell you that everything you write, speak, and plan for in your vision will happen the moment you execute the principles. Unfortunately, this is not true, but in truth, *delay* is a necessary part of the vision process. Thus, it's not unfortunate; it's necessary.

Your mind is a powerful tool for manifestation. Proverbs 23:7 says, *"For as* [a man] *thinketh in his heart, so is he."* Where your life is right now is a direct result of the thoughts of your past. Therefore, if you can begin to change your thoughts, you can actually transform your life.

This is also a salient point because of the power of your mind. It's impossible to control all of the some sixty thousand thoughts that flow through your head on a daily basis. Each one of these thoughts carries with it the power and potential to manifest in your life. So, delay is important. It gives you time to evaluate your thinking so you only bring into your life those things that God wants for you, and not the many unstoppable negative thoughts you will inevitably think in a day. The key is to catch these thoughts and make self-correction, and therefore, alignment in your thoughts and mind. Thus, the first challenge to your vision is time. You have to be able to deal with the inevitable delays that will come when you make faith-filled moves ignited by vision.

To deal properly with the concept of delay, we must understand time. One thing that fascinates me about Albert Einstein, and other quantum physicists, is the way they view time. For them, time is an illusion. They understand time as a continuum—something that is happening simultaneously and all at once. From this perspective, you already have the things you desire before you even receive them. This is why your confessions should always be stated as, "I am *now.*" We speak them in the now because we believe that what we're speaking out of our mouth is already a settled matter. Even Mark 11:24 tells us that we should believe that we receive. So, when you pray, you should pray as if you have already received what you desire. That's how true prayer works. It acknowledges that time is an illusion, a continuum, and one in which you can say that you already have what you desire even before it manifests.

This, to me, is the essence of faith. It's the ability to believe something before it happens. Dr. Martin Luther King Jr. said, "Take the first step in faith. You don't have to see the whole staircase, just take the first step." This, then, becomes our challenge with time. Can we continue to confess what we desire even if the way isn't made clear? If we can do that, then we can overcome the obstacle of delay.

I don't, for a second, want you to think that facing the challenge of delay is an easy task. You're working against mental conditioning that predates you. We all have a rich history of failure, setback, and doubt. We all have voices from the past that speak to us in the present. At times, those ancient voices can shout so loudly that they talk you out of your future. Then, when something is delayed longer than the allotted time that we've anticipated, we convince ourselves that this faith stuff doesn't work, and we abandoned the dream just before it comes to fruition.

Your history and programming are working against you. You have to set your mind on what you believe instead of what you see. *"Faith is the substance of things hoped for, the evidence of things not seen,"* the apostle Paul tells us in Hebrews 11:1. You must become so intimately acquainted with your vision that, no matter what happens between the time you release your vision and the time it actually manifests, you remain unwavering in your resolve.

You have to access the unbreakable concept of *hope*. It's hope that keeps us moving forward, allowing us to maintain our sanity until we can see a better future. Hope is the backbone to belief. It's a foundational element that keeps you holding on, even when things seem impossible. In fact, many times, I have had to hold on to my hope when it seemed that my dream was retreating in the opposite direction of what I was believing for. The amazing thing about hope is the effect it has on your psyche when, in the face of insurmountable odds, you remain in a place of receiving. Hope, in Hebrews 11:1, is the Greek word *elpizo*, which means, "to wait for salvation with joy and full confidence." This verse not only deals with soteriology, which is the doctrine of salvation, but it also applies to the different situations we face in this life. We have to find our place of joy, and full confidence, even when it seems as if it's not working. Easy for me to say! No, it's not an easy process. In fact, it's supremely difficult to look at a fledgling business and still hold out hope that it's going to work. Anxiety can overwhelm you when you're facing the possible destruction of all that you've worked for, and yet, you're still holding on to hope.

> The amazing thing about hope is the effect it has on your psyche when, in the face of insurmountable odds, you remain in a place of receiving.

I can't help but think of the movie *Rudy* when I ponder this concept. It was the true story of a guy who was undersized, had no family support in the way of belief, and wasn't even a student at Notre Dame, yet he believed he would one day make the football team. It was an impossible dream, and yet it happened. It happened when he felt like quitting; it happened in his darkest hour; it happened when it looked hopeless. In the depths of mental anguish, he made that team.

You too can access the power of hope. You too can have confidence when everyone around you is telling you to quit. You can draw on a strength deep within to maintain and keep a high level of hope.

As I'm writing this chapter, I'm thirty thousand feet in the air, and, for some reason, I have one song on repeat going from my phone into my wireless headphones. I don't know why, but from the moment I walked into the airport, I felt compelled to listen to "Rise Up" by Andra Day. This one line keeps speaking to me: "I'll rise up, and I'll do it a thousand times." That's the place you have to come to; that no matter how many times you fall down, you have to keep getting back up again. I want you to know that, no matter how far down you get, all you need is hope.

One of the Hebrew translations of *hope* is "a cord," and the connotation is that of a rope. Sometimes that's all you need. You need a rope of hope, something you can hold on to. You may be at the end of that rope, but don't let go. Even in your most difficult times, you've never been closer to everything working out. Another translation of the Greek word for *hope* is "an expectation of good." That's the essence of what I'm trying to convey here. Can you, in the face of defeat, still expect good to show up? If you can, then your hope will be rewarded by producing the very thing you're believing God for.

Keep hope alive even in a seemingly hopeless situation. By doing this, you will keep yourself focused on the outcome. That's a major part of success: being able to ignore what looks contrary to your vision, including the time it takes for it to manifest.

When you're challenged with the inevitable delay that comes when you activate your faith in your vision, I want you to take heart. Center yourself with hope, because your faith is the substance of things hoped for. Keep hope alive even in a seemingly hopeless situation. By doing this, you will keep yourself focused on the outcome. That's a major part of success: being able to ignore what looks contrary to your vision, including the time it takes for it to manifest. Keep picturing success and eventually what you see is what you'll be.

The Challenge of How

Another obstacle to vision is an obvious one. At some point in this book, you've probably said to yourself, *All this sounds good, but how am I going to do it?* A major challenge to the vision process is focusing on the *how* instead of the *why*.

Friedrich Nietzsche said, "He who has a why to love for can bear almost any how." This statement is never truer than when you are waiting for your vision to manifest in material form. Our natural inclination is to wonder *how* something is going to happen. This, however, is a hindrance to the vision we hold in our minds and in our hearts. It has never been, and will never be, about *how*. It will always be about *why*. You must be so convinced of the *why* that the *how* has no other choice but to occur. The crucial point is that your vision must be centered in your passion. Your central focus must be "Why do I want this?" or "Why do I do this?"

I recently saw a commercial for an insurance company. It began by showing a picture of a soldier in uniform. His voice narrated, saying, "I was a mechanic in the Marines." The scene then shifts to a garage and the soldier wearing a mechanics outfit, saying, "I feel at home when I get my hands dirty." Now this is a man living his passion. For me, the last thing I want to do is work on a car and get greasy hands, but for him, that is his bliss. You have to find your bliss, your greatest joy, and pursue it with all your heart. You can't focus on the how because the how is never clear. You must focus on your why. "I do this because I love it." "This is what brings me fulfillment." When you follow that path, your *how* will always show up.

You see, the *how*'s always take care of themselves, and many of them are beyond your control. You're going to need favor that only God can give, and you're going to need situations to come into harmony that you have no power to perform on your own. When you follow your passion, there is a lot of guesswork involved, because faith often isn't laid out for you in a step-by-step fashion. You have to walk it out, one step at a time, and keep moving forward. Remember, your *how* will always present itself, and it often comes in an unexpected manner. Vision is all about expectation, but you have to know that God will do things that will completely blow your mind. He will defy the odds, tip the scales in your favor, and, quite frankly, bend rules for you. I want you to overcome the challenge of *how* by falling in love with your *why*. When you're focused on *why*, the *how* will reveal itself and the path will be made clear.

> When you follow your passion, there is a lot of guesswork involved, because faith often isn't laid out for you in a step-by-step fashion. You have to walk it out, one step at a time, and keep moving forward.

The reason your *why* is so important is because it gets to the core of who you are. It causes you to focus on what really matters, your internal reasons and motivations. If you do something only for fame or recognition, it will be a fleeting manifestation. When you do what you do from the heart, it produces humility, not hubris. More than 2,500 years ago, Lao-Tzu wrote *Tao Te Ching*, in which he said, "All streams flow to the sea because it is lower than they are. Humility gives it its power." When you're centered on why you do something instead of what it can produce, you become humbled by the process. This empowers you like the ocean. Because the ocean is low, all rivers flow to it. It doesn't have to beg, fight, or demand anything. The rivers willingly come to it because it remains low. Your *why* should put you in this state of ease and awareness. I can remember the tears that streamed down my face the first time I received an opportunity to speak on a major platform. I was so humbled by the experience, and the chance to actually do what I love in front of a massive crowd. It made me feel so thankful, and because of that, more opportunities followed, because I stayed low.

Take the focus off the *how*. Live from your heart; live from your passion; make a declaration that you will love what you do and do what you love. The word *amateur* comes from a Latin word meaning "for the love of." Let us always keep an amateur's heart, even when we're being paid to do what we do. Do it because you love it, operate from that deep internal *why*, and you'll never have to worry about the *how*.

The Challenge of Fear

One of my favorite quotes comes from, in my opinion, one of the only true theologians of the twentieth century: Paul Tillich. He said, "Doubt is not the opposite of faith; it is one element of faith." What an incredible thought. All my life, I was told that faith and fear couldn't cohabitate. I was taught that faith and fear can't share the same space. When I first read Tillich's statement, it seemed to resonate with me. It made sense, because I knew from personal experience that each time I stepped out on faith, I would be inundated with thoughts and feelings of fear and doubt. I saw the validity of his words, because if you really think about it, real faith should create fear. We should dream so big that we doubt if it can come true, which in turn causes us to completely rely on God to bring it to pass. When I once taught on this topic, I named my message, "If you're not scared, you're not doing it right." True challenges to our faith level naturally produce fear.

I want you to understand fear instead of abhorring it. Fear comes with the territory of faith. If you have a God-given vision, you will experience fear. Learn to harness what fear affords you. Fear reveals the areas in which you need to strengthen your faith. It also serves to remind you that there are some things in your life that only God can do.

We must learn to embrace fear, and then turn it on itself. One way to accomplish this is to use something we discussed in previous chapters: *contrast*. You will feel fear, especially when you start to launch your vision—it's inevitable. The key is to contrast the fear and not to fuel it. This is done in the same way you form your confessions of faith. You ask yourself, *What do I want?* Then you take the attention off your fear and focus on what you're believing for. This can help to shift your thoughts from what you don't want to what you do want.

This doesn't work with all fear, because some of the fear we have is on a subconscious level. Our subconscious mind controls most of our daily activity. It's always there, running silent scripts that affect our everyday lives. Many of them are unconscious fears that were downloaded into our minds at a young age. For these types of fears, we have to go deeper than the simple process of contrast.

I can tell you with pinpoint accuracy one of my subconscious thoughts that was deposited into me at a young age. I was always told, and shown, that my family never had enough money. I like to tell the story of my toys. I didn't have that many, and most of the ones I had were given to me as gifts. The few toys I had never had batteries. When I would go to a friend's house, I would always assume that their toys didn't work either. But to my surprise, they actually had batteries and did work! My toys never had batteries because we were always too broke to buy something as expensive as batteries. When we went to the store, if I asked for some gum or candy, I was always told that we didn't have enough money for that. This was probably a true statement. But I want you to understand what that did to my subconscious programming. This idea of lack and not having enough became ingrained in my subconscious mind, and as an adult, I saw it manifest in my life. In fact, there was a season in my life when I was making good money, but I constantly found myself back at zero. No matter how much money I made, at some point, I would always be broke again. This was because I was plagued with this idea that I would never have enough—an idea I never created but was given to me.

Just as faith attracts what you're believing for, fear attracts what you're afraid of. That's why it's so important that you deal with the subconscious fears of your past.

This notion dogged me until I started taking a deeper look at my core beliefs. You can do this by taking an area of fear or lack and asking yourself some questions about it. Fear is a magnet. Just as faith attracts what you're believing for, fear attracts what you're afraid of. That's why it's so important that you deal with the subconscious fears of your past. You can begin by looking at an area that you fear or are unsuccessful in, especially the negative things you habitually find yourself doing. Ask yourself, *Where did this fear or behavior come from?* This is also a powerful tool for overcoming addictions and habits. By recognizing when these habits started, you can began to unravel the physiological baggage that has attached itself to you over time. Now you are getting to the source of the problem.

For me, the source was always experiencing lack in my childhood, and being told that we never had enough money. Throughout my life, money was something I had to work long and hard for, but still I never had enough. I first started to dismantle the thought that you have to work hard for money in my early twenties. In the Army, there's a saying: "Work smarter, not harder." I heard this so many times when I was in the service, but I was always in the position of doing the opposite. I was working harder, not smarter. It wasn't until I learned how to position myself for better jobs that I was able to make conscious decisions to work smarter and not harder. By the time I got out of the military, instead of going to the field and working at the motor pool all day, which were difficult jobs, I secured a position in the medical records room and was able to work in a clinical setting and eventually ran the entire department by myself. I had no one watching over me and I was free from the rigorous work of the normal soldier. I even did this early in my career by securing a special position at the hospital teaching emergency medicine instead of being with the tanker battalion I was assigned to. I started to learn that you could do what you want and make the same pay as those who were doing more difficult work. As I prepared to leave the military, I decided that I never wanted to work for another person again. So I read books like *The 7 Habits of Highly Effective People* by Stephen

Covey. I read books on real estate investing, and anything that had to do with wealth. In this way, I was gaining outside information that was in stark contrast to what I had been conditioned to think. But these actions only came after I began to understand the origin of the lie I believed—that there is never enough money to go around. In truth, there is plenty of money to go around, but too many of us have become products of our environment and upbringing. We adopted someone else's reality until it became our reality. Only by pinpointing when this began can we begin to unravel the many untrue and negative thoughts that are holding us back.

I have already mentioned the second thing you must do. After you identify the origin of the thoughts, you must take in new information. The only way to effectively remove former thoughts is by introducing newer ones to your subconscious. I didn't have mentors growing up, and I never felt like I needed one. I really thought that I knew all I needed to know, and that I could make it in this world by myself. This came from being fatherless, then having a stepfather who made no investment in me and considered me to be the baggage of his relationship. To make things even more difficult, my mother took his side and never stood up for me. This caused me to be rebellious against authority, because I didn't trust it and it had only brought me pain. This made it difficult for anyone to get close to me or make an impact in my life. Since authority brought me pain, I rebelled against all authority. It wasn't until I got older that I started to realize the importance of mentors. It started with my football and wrestling coaches, then my pastor, and finally my platoon sergeant in the Army. All of these people played great roles in my life as mentors and helped me to develop as a person. After the military, I was once again left without a role model. So, I gained information from books I read. Great authors became my mentors and I gleaned their information to adjust my thinking and impregnate myself with new thoughts that ultimately became my new core beliefs.

> When you change negative and limiting ways of thinking, you start a process that will eventually change the way you act. When your new thoughts became new actions, you're setting yourself up for transformation.

Finally, you must use repetition. This is why I teach that confessions are an important part of the vision process. Repetition changes the make-up of your thoughts. When you repeatedly say something, you simultaneously hear what you're saying. This gets at the core of your beliefs and you start to think in the way you desire instead of the ways in which you've been taught. It is similar to an athlete developing muscle memory. Whether it's a wrestling move, a golf or baseball swing, or designed play on the football field, repetition is the key to make doing the right thing an automatic impulse in your life. In many ways, and without realizing it, you've already been working on automatic all this time, using the scripts you inherited from your parents and your upbringing. To change those thoughts, you must discover where they came from, gain new information, and then repeat the new information until new thoughts and actions become second nature. We're all creatures of habit. That's why it's so important that we form better habits by challenging and, if necessary, changing our core beliefs. When you change negative and limiting ways of thinking, you start a process that will eventually change the way you act. When your new thoughts became new actions, you're setting yourself up for transformation. In time, you will shift from fear to faith by understanding, facing, and working with your fear.

The Challenge of Feeling Unworthy

One of the greatest challenges to vision is the feeling of unworthiness. In Romans 12:2, Paul says, *"Be not conformed to this world...."* *Conformed* is the Greek word *syschematizo*, which means "to conform one's self (one's mind and character) to another's pattern." I really tried to look at this word and see how it applied to real-life circumstances. I believe that Paul is telling us to be authentic. That we shouldn't fashion ourselves after the pattern of other people. That we need to be the authentic, unique person we were created to be. I believe that we were all placed on this planet to fulfill a purpose, and we all benefit when we do what we were purposed to do. Paul is telling us to be ourselves and not pattern ourselves after others.

As I'm writing this chapter, my birthday is two days away. I'll turn forty-three. I've recently realized that I'm just now learning who I really am. It has taken me some time to work through certain things in my life. I have always been a person who keeps pushing forward, no matter what. I've been outwardly action-oriented and not really inwardly emotion-oriented. In all my forward progression, there are certain things in my life that I never took the time and energy to deal with in order to more fully develop into who God wants me to be. There were people I had to forgive, things I had to let go of, and truths I needed to discover about myself. It wasn't until I faced the things I had been ignoring for so long that I really started to come into myself. For so many of us, there are certain insecurities and mistakes in our past that hinder us from reaching our full potential. This will cause us to *"conform,"* as Paul says, to patterns that are not authentic to who we are. This is significant because you were uniquely created by God, and it's only when we can reveal our authentic selves that we can truly be free and feel worthy of all that God has for us.

Paul also tells us directly what we shouldn't be conformed to *"this world."* This is significant because *"world"* in this verse is the Greek word *aion*, which is simply a "period of time." This word is also associated with the past in relation to time. As I mentioned before, we must change our relationship and connection to the past. It's imperative that we accept the past. Your past is as much a part of you as anything else, but we don't have to have our future dictated by our past.

While I was traveling recently, my driver kept telling me how stupid he was in his twenties, and about all the bad decisions he had made. I shifted his thinking and told him that he should celebrate the mistakes of his past, simply because he wouldn't be who he is today without those periods of learning in his life. Psalm 139:14 says we are *"fearfully and wonderfully made."* It seems so strange to think that we have been *"fearfully"* made. In Hebrew, it is the word *yare*, and one of its meanings is "to stand in awe." Before God created you, He did a review of your life and, since He's all-knowing, He already knew every mistake, every failure, as well as every victory in your life—even the ones you haven't experienced yet! In light of all this, God stepped back and stood in awe of what He had created—you. What an empowering thought to imagine that God, knowing all our future mistakes, would still be in awe of us. I want you to know that you are worthy of God's love and His blessing. You can reach your goals in life, and God is behind you, pushing you forward the entire time. Even in all the challenges that have come and will come, you must realize how special you are to God. Your past is a part of your story, but it doesn't have to be the end of your story. It has taken me some time to overcome the pain of my past, but just as I have done it, so can you do it too. Don't get stuck in a place that you can never return to. You can't go back, so let it go! You have to face it, accept it, put it aside, and move forward. I know this is easier said than done, but trust me, it *can* be done. Slowly, daily, you can heal and become stronger, regardless of your past. This is significant to learn, because your past makes up the sum total of who you are, and you'll never feel worthy as long as you remain living in the past.

To do this, it may help to break down the past into workable parts. I have come to realize that not everything can be easily placed under theological jurisdiction and simply vanish. There are things that have happened to you that are not your fault. Someone hurt, abused, or mistreated you, and it has nothing to do with your worthiness. In Jordan B. Peterson's book *12 Rules for Life: An Antidote to Chaos*, he makes a very interesting point. He points to Genesis and the relationship between Abel and God. God loved Abel, found him acceptable, and was connected to him. Yet, this relationship didn't stop Cain from killing Abel. The point I draw from this is that you can be in close quarters with God and still not be immune to the actions of other people. At some point, people in your life, in their free will, chose to violate you in a myriad of ways, and there's no way to get around that. It's wrong and it will have damaging effects on your future if not properly dealt with.

> You can be in close quarters with God and still not be immune to the actions of other people. At some point, people in your life, in their free will, chose to violate you in a myriad of ways, and there's no way to get around that. It's wrong and it will have damaging effects on your future if not properly dealt with.

If we're ever going to feel worthy of our dreams, we must deal with this aspect of our past. The most powerful tool I've found is forgiveness. I've always been a person (I thought) who could easily forgive. This has been true in most areas of my life, but I especially found it difficult with my family. The reason this was such a challenge was because the person who hurt me never apologized. This means I had to forgive someone who was unrepentant. That's tough for anyone! How do you forgive the unremorseful? It took me some time, but I realized that unforgiveness is like drinking poison and waiting for the other person to die. A Chinese proverb says that if you're going to insist on getting revenge, you'd better dig two graves. This simply means that in trying to kill the other person, you will also be killing yourself.

Listen, you have a right to be upset, but in the end, you're only hurting yourself. You have to let it all go. There is freedom for you when you can do this. It will bring you to your authentic self by removing what happened to you so you can begin to enjoy what's happening now. Most of us live in two places we have never been, the past and the future, when, in all actuality, the only thing we have power to change is the present. This is why it's so important to find out who you are and what you have the potential to become by removing your focus from the past and the future, and centering it on the here and now.

I want to encourage you and let you know that challenges are always an indication that you're on the right path. You're going to be challenged regardless of what you do in this life. Why not be challenged in doing something great?

There's a quote that has been attributed to both Winston Churchill and Abraham Lincoln. While scholars have dismissed both of them as the true author, regardless of who said it, the quote is transformative and should be the standard we reach for when challenged in our dreams. The quote states, "Success is going from failure to failure without losing your enthusiasm." Enthusiasm comes from the Greek words *en-* and *-theos*, literally meaning to be "in God." One way to know whether or not you're in the Spirit is to check your level of enthusiasm in the face of failure. You have to accept that setbacks are a part of the process, the key to never giving up. You must keep rising up, over and over again, and eventually, you will obtain your dreams. Face the challenges in life that come against your vision and champion on, knowing that you will win if you just don't quit.

FINAL THOUGHTS

NINE

FINAL THOUGHTS

As we look over this journey learning the principles that govern faith and how to manifest the vision of God for your life, it's important to remember a few things. The first thing I want you to know is that you don't have to be limited by your past experiences. Your past talks with a megaphone and tries to talk you out of your future. If your past experiences are allowed to dominate your present self-talk, then you will continue to be what you have always been and do what you have always done. That's why it's so important in the beginning of the vision process to tell yourself it's all right to dream. Tell yourself that you don't have to live the way you have always lived. Know that you can imagine a greater life for yourself. There are no limits with God; you are not limited. You serve a God of infinite possibilities, and He wants to show His awesome power in your life. You have to be willing to put the past aside long enough to imagine a better future. My greatest advice when you start this process is to dream as big as you can. See if you can upgrade your first thought to something even bigger. God will do more than you can ask or think (see Ephesians 3:20), so don't sell yourself short. Take out a sheet of paper or open a document on your computer to write out in detail every aspect of your life that you want to change. What does your spiritual life, family life, home life, job life, and possessions look like from this elevated place of vision? Write it all out in detail, dreaming as big as you can.

Next, write out your goals. This is where you take the large dream and condense it into workable targets, so you have something to work with. Then write your goals as positive confessions. You see, your goals are a target for your mind, but speaking your goals as affirmations changes your thoughts. That's what makes confessions so powerful. When you change your thoughts, you change your life. Remember that you can also find Scriptures that deal with what you are dreaming about or wish to change. With Scriptures you can form confessions that take the Word and make it a part of your everyday experience and a part of your normal thought life.

> When you change your thoughts,
> you change your life.

After you have written out these confessions, it's time to write out the plans and steps you intend to take to see your dreams become a reality. This is when the proverbial rubber meets the road. This is when you form your mission statement, which is your highest reason for doing what you do; your three subgoals, which support the overall goal; and strategies for how you will accomplish them.

I have written this book not only so you can live a life of joy and excitement but so that you can truly feel the exhilaration of living a purposeful, intentional life. This book is about coming in contact with God in a new way, living for God and not just existing, and extending this experience to others. This book is also about love—love of God, family, and the short time we have here to live our lives. I pray that you would not only experience the full impact of this teaching on vision but that you would also apply the principles and understand that it all works by love. God wants to bring your vision to pass because He loves you, He wants to see you happy and fulfilled, and He wants to see you share this

Final Thoughts 185

same experience and love with every person that crosses your path. You were created to live a life of joy and abundance.

Sadly, for many of us, our experiences have been nothing close to this. We have been hit with sickness, lack, pain, depression, and distress on every hand. Our minds are so flooded with the negative aspects of our lives that the thought of it ever being different is choked out before it even gets a chance to be planted. Thankfully, we can change that by writing out our vision. You don't have to live in the old patterns passed down to you and the learned behaviors of your life experience. You are free to dream and to do that on the largest scale possible. God has given you a vivid and powerful imagination. You can imagine what life can look like in your future. You can imagine something better for you and your family. With the tools provided in this book, you can not only imagine it, but you take the necessary steps to see it through. You can see yourself being healthy and enjoying a long life of health. You can see yourself enjoying your life pain-free. You can see it and speak it every day. You can plan for it through writing and see your body transformed into a healthy, fully functioning entity that is here to serve you as you live out your days. You can imagine that you don't have to live paycheck to paycheck and that you can live in abundance from the source of super abundance and life, which is God. You can speak it every day and watch your mind be renewed and transformed into something new and different. Then your thoughts and words of abundance can become the plans that will put action to your faith and give you the necessary steps to take to live out your life of abundance.

> You don't have to live in the old patterns passed down to you and the learned behaviors of your life experience. You are free to dream and to do that on the largest scale possible. God has given you a vivid and powerful imagination. You can imagine what life can look like in your future.

I truly believe that the most important thing people can do once they have accepted Christ as their Savior is to find out what their purpose is. After finding that purpose, they can write out a vision to see that purpose come to pass. I want you to know that you will become what you do or do not plan to become. If you live your life without a vision, you are subject to default and whatever comes your way. However, if you take a leap by dreaming the highest dream you can, writing it down, forming your goals, creating your confessions, and planning for the accomplishment of your vision, you will find that life has so much more to offer. You can do, be, and have whatever you put your focus on. If you want to travel the world, you can do it! Put it in your vision. If you want to go to college, you can do it! Write it in your vision. If you want to start a business, you can do it! Write it in your vision. Send that powerful message into the spirit realm, that you will have what you intend, that you will become all that God has called you to be, and that nothing will hold you back from living the life you have envisioned.

I have given you time-tested biblical tools to change the course of your life. It's time to connect with God and find out what awesome plans He has for you. Don't waste another minute of your life wondering what you will do. You have the knowledge, tools, and, most importantly, God. You will succeed as you apply these principles in your life. I believe that God led you to this book for a reason. Perhaps you feel a sense that God is calling you to a higher place. This place is before you now. Take this book and all it teaches and apply it to your life. If you do, you will see phenomenal transformation.

I pray that from this day forward, your life will never be the same. I pray that everything you dream will come to pass in your life, starting from this very moment on.

ABOUT THE AUTHOR

ABOUT THE AUTHOR

Shane Perry Sr. is a man of focus and vision, who is known for his love of people and passion for ministry. He travels the world preaching a message of hope and teaching the masses how to find God's purpose for their life.

Dr. Perry has incredible insight and teaches practical ways to find God's purpose in everyday life. He has preached at some of the largest churches, conferences, corporate events, and television networks of our generation. In October 2013, he received his Doctorate of Divinity from Richmond Virginia Seminary. Dr. Perry has hosted *Praise the Lord* on Trinity Broadcasting Network, and has also been featured on several other networks, such as Black Entertainment Television and the Inspiration Network.

His philanthropic work includes programs designed to help the mentally disabled, fatherless, and displaced. In addition, Dr. Perry is a dedicated family man. He is happily married to Latoiya Perry, and they are the proud parents of Shane Jr., Autumn, Lauren, and Jaxon.